A FORGE OF FREEDOM BOOK

0 50 100 200 MILES
N
W
E
S
Ticonderoga
N.H.
Portsmouth
Boston
Plymouth
NEW YORK
Albany
MASS.
Hartford
R.I.
CONN.
Newport
New Haven
Providence
N.Y.
N.J.
New York City
PENNSYLVANIA
Trenton
Burlington
Philadelphia
Wilmington
Baltimore
Annapolis
DEL.
MD.
MD.
VIRGINIA
Richmond
Williamsburg
Jamestown
ATLANTIC OCEAN
NORTH CAROLINA
New Bern
Charlotte
Wilmington
SOUTH CAROLINA
Charleston
GEORGIA
Savannah
The Thirteen Colonies
1763
RIKI

The Massachusetts Colony

by

ROBERT SMITH

Crowell-Collier Press, New York, New York
COLLIER-MACMILLAN PUBLISHERS, LONDON

Acknowledgment

This book could not have been written without the generous assistance of the staffs of the Boston Atheneum and the Lenox (Massachusetts) Public Library

Library of Congress Catalog Card Number: 69-19575

The Macmillan Company
866 Third Avenue, New York, N.Y. 10022
Collier-Macmillan Canada Ltd., Toronto, Ontario
Printed in the United States of America

10 9 8 7 6 5 4 3

PICTURE CREDITS
The Bettmann Archive, Inc., 13, 31, 72, 123, 130–31; Culver Pictures, Inc., 3, 28, 57, 84, 104, 117, 138; Historical Pictures Service–Chicago, 6, 10, 18, 24, 27, 36, 40, 48, 63, 68, 78–79, 92, 97, 100, 110, 112–13.

COVER ILLUSTRATION: *The Battle of Lexington*

To five of my favorite history students:

Linda Jones
Kathie O'Neill
Katie Rowe
Nora Smith
Allison Van Leer

Contents

1 The First Settlers

For more than a hundred years before the Pilgrims sailed their tiny ship into the great bay above Cape Cod, seeking a pleasant place to settle, there had been English fishermen and traders working all up and down the New England coast. Some men believe that fishermen from Bristol, England, had reached Newfoundland and Cape Breton before Columbus ever set sail from Spain.

So when people on the *Mayflower* established their first colony, and named it Plymouth, they already knew something of what the sea and the land might hold. They knew that there was fertile soil here, with bountiful fishing, friendly natives, rich pasture, and timber and furs. Just the same, they were surprised almost out of their wits when a tall Indian chief named Sam-o-Set strode down the middle of their little settlement, only a few months after it had been built, crying "Welcome Englishmen! Welcome Englishmen!" A straight, proud man, with black hair that fell down his back, a wildcat skin thrown over his shoulder and long buckskin stockings on his legs, Sam-o-Set carried himself like a king. And the Pilgrims, halting their work, or running to their doorways to see him, watched him open-mouthed. Only God, they must have told themselves, could have inspired this savage to speak in the English tongue.

But the Indians who dwelt along the shores of Massachusetts had dealt with Englishmen all their lives. They had traded their furs to Englishmen for blankets and cloth and things made out of metal, and they had showed the

Englishmen how to dry fish and where to find clams. Some Indians even sailed to England with returning traders and there learned enough English to describe the wonders of the new world to marveling lords and ladies. The stories they told, as well as their own noble and vigorous appearance, tempted more men to come look into this wilderness that, at Captain John Smith's suggestion, the king had decided to call New England.

The very first Englishmen who had come this way, in a ship captained by an Italian they called John Cabot, had been seeking gold and silver and rare spices. The British king had no money to spend merely looking for a place to fish. But fish was to remain the real treasure of Massachusetts for a long time to come. Even after the Revolution had set the colonies free, the peace treaty was delayed because the Americans would not yield up their right to fish everywhere off their coasts.

John Smith, however, saw much more than fish in Massachusetts. The Indians, he noted, traveled far to the west, even to certain great lakes, to find otter and beaver. Almost any crop could thrive in the soil, and cattle would grow fat. The timber was rich and there was stone of every kind, for building or for making forges. He was sure too that there was enough iron to provide all the fittings they needed to build ships here. The Indians grew corn aplenty, enough to trade it off with their more northerly neighbors. The country of the Massachusetts (a tribe of Indians), said John Smith, "is the Paradise of all those parts: for here are many isles all planted with corn; groves, mulberries, savage gardens, and good harbors: the Coast is for the most part high clayey sandy cliffs. The Sea Coast as you pass shows you all along large corn fields and great troupes of well proportioned people."

Knowing all these things awaited them, the Pilgrims were not too fearful as they set about, in the summer of 1620, to build themselves a new and permanent home,

By 1622 Plymouth Colony was an established community of sturdy log houses and cleared fields

where they would have, as they said, "purity of conscience and liberty of worship." But neither John Smith nor any others had told them how long and how bitterly cold the winters were. No matter how much wood they had cut and piled and no matter how much food they had harvested and stored, they did not have enough to last them all the way to spring. Only the kindness of the Indians, in sharing their food and in showing the Puritans the next season how to plant crops that would grow best in this land, saved the little colony. Even at that, many grew sick and died, for lack of warmth and enough to eat.

Plymouth Colony, for the first sixty years or more, was not the same as Massachusetts Bay. John Smith counted it part of Virginia, the southernmost of the king's colonies on these shores. It was not until some five years later, when some noblemen seeking the riches John Smith and the Indian captives had told about, tried to establish settlements a little farther up the coast (but still behind the long protecting arm of Cape Cod) that the Colony of Massachusetts Bay began to take shape.

The first to land, after the Pilgrims had settled at Plymouth, established themselves at the spot now called Weymouth, then later at Salem, which was called Naumkeag by the Indians. Many of these settlers gave up after their first bitter winter and returned to England. But a few clung to the new land, some living in misery and patiently praying for help to arrive from home, and others learning to trade with the Indians and make their own way. Then a well-planned voyage was made, bringing several shiploads of people who longed to escape the tyranny of the English bishops and the highhandedness of Charles I. Unlike the Pilgrims, who were "separatists," these men and women never thought of themselves as deserting the Church of England. They sought only freedom to reform it, in accordance with their consciences, and they maintained communication with it and thought of it as the mother church.

This company carried the original charter of Massachusetts Bay. They were well-supplied, to begin with, but were discouraged by the scenes of starvation and disease they found at Salem. They moved a little to the south and settled at a spot by a river mouth and named it Charlestown, after the king. But the lack of fresh water brought sickness and death there and the newcomers nearly despaired. Then a man who had been living a lonely life in a small hut just across the river from this settlement, in a stretch of sparsely wooded land almost surrounded by water, learned of their plight and came to invite them to his own land. This was William Blackstone, one of those who first landed at Weymouth but who, instead of going home, had built himself a small cabin on the slope of a hill in this place the Indians called Sha-wata-muc or Shawmut. He lived there all by himself, tending a small garden and an apple orchard, safe from wolves and bears because of the water that surrounded him and the lack of forest on this stretch of land. There was a fine spring almost at his doorstep, and the king had granted him all this land for his own.

The leader of the new arrivals, John Winthrop, a strong-minded and well-to-do man who had been told he was "too old" (at forty-two) to start a new colony, accepted Blackstone's invitation. Almost all the company came over with him to the place that they had called Trimountaine (because of the three hills they could see looking across from Charlestown). They even brought the frame for Winthrop's new house that they had already begun to build at Charlestown. And they decided to name the settlement Boston, after the English home of one of their beloved neighbors, Arbella Johnson, who had died in the first few weeks after landing at Charlestown.

Like the men and women who had come first to Plymouth, these settlers too hoped for "purity of conscience." To that end, they wanted to elect their own ministers and not have them named by tyrannical bishops. Their charter, giving permission to settle and own this land (which belonged to the English crown because John Cabot had discovered it), gave them many rights that later kings wished had never been granted. The most important was the right to select their own minister. Their community was a religious one entirely. They did not come to grant to other people freedom to worship as they pleased. They sought that freedom only for themselves and they seriously believed they were there to establish a sort of Kingdom of God, or of the Saints, with only those who professed the true religion allowed to take part.

It is difficult to find men and women today, outside of a convent or a monastery, who fill their lives as full of religion as those Puritan settlers did. They gave thanks every day, and many times a day, to their God for all His blessings, great and small. If they set sail for an island in

The Puritans were pious people who devoted what little leisure time they had to meditation, prayer, and worship

the bay and the wind was blowing in the wrong direction, they assumed that God did not want them to reach that destination. When they started on a journey, they put themselves in God's hands, and they thanked Him for safe arrival. For they were convinced that God's chief concern was the safety and security of His most devoted servants—themselves. They even gave thanks to God when they found that smallpox had wiped out most of the Indians along the Massachusetts coast near Boston, thereby providing much abandoned land, including the very spot where Boston was built. This, they confidently declared, was just a further sign of God's desire that they should settle in this land and have room to multiply.

The Puritans sought to please God and remain in communion with Him through their "works"—that is, leading a life devoted to hard work, meditation, prayer, and worship, without concern for trifles such as pretty clothes, laughter, games, amusements, sweets, and delicate things to eat. Their clothes and food were plain. They worked long hours. They refrained from work and travel on the Sabbath. They attended "meeting" (that is, church services) several times a week. For recreation, they would go to the Great and Thursday Lecture at the meeting house, where they would be instructed in religious matters or inspired by one of their religious leaders.

The Puritan Sabbath was far more severe than many people realize. It was more than a day of rest. Beginning at sundown on Saturday, each family was expected to devote itself to prayer, contemplation, and the reading of the Gospel. They were not to labor, take naps, or even go for a stroll. They were not to chat with the neighbors. In Boston the city gates (on narrow Boston Neck) were shut and the ferries closed down so that no one could leave the town. The citizens could not wander by the harbor or the river, or even seek in summer the green coolness of an open field. If three or four men and women should meet in the street and stop to exchange pleasantries, the tithesman would be upon them to keep them moving toward home or toward the meeting house. (The tithesman—or tenthsman—was selected to be responsible for the moral and religious behavior of ten families.) Even as recently as fifty years ago in New England, should anyone be heard hammering inside his house, or be observed pulling weeds in his garden, the neighbors might call the police. And only a few decades ago a guest in a small New England summer hotel who heard laughter and the slapping down of playing cards in the room next to his might hasten to complain to the management that there were Sabbath-breakers in the house.

Men who fell out of favor with the minister and elders of the church suffered in many ways. Under the original charter—which was just a written agreement between the colonists and the king setting forth what powers the king had and what rights the colonists held on to—the vote in all colony elections was restricted to "freemen." But that word had a special meaning. A "freeman" in Massachusetts was a citizen who was in good standing in the Puritan (Congregational) Church. Unless a man had a letter from his minister declaring that he was fulfilling his religious duties, he could not vote at all. And so the church controlled not only religious affairs but all the lawmaking machinery of the whole colony.

Naturally, with the increase in the number of men and women who either did not belong to the Congregational Church or did not live up to its strictest standards, there was much discontent. Men who ran shops or worked at trades or owned farms wanted to have some voice in choosing the men who might tax them or set hours for their work or decide about protecting them from the Indians. And many of the leaders of the Congregational Church could see the justice in these desires. The tradition of democracy, or choosing one's own leaders and making the laws one had to live by, did not make sense if it was limited to a small sect.

There were other traditions that made Massachusetts very different from some of the other colonies. When a new town was to be formed in the colony, it was required to provide for a Congregational minister and for a school. When a township was marked off (six square miles making a township), there had to be a certain portion of land that no individual could own—room for the meeting house and for the school. To this day, in the wilds of Maine, where many townships have been marked off but have not yet been developed, almost any woodsman can show you the "school lot"—a portion of the wilderness that must remain in public hands so that a school may be built there some day. Maine was a part of Massachusetts for many years and still retains many of the same traditions.

The town meeting was another Massachusetts tradition that helped instil in all who were born or came to live there the habit of giving one's opinion out loud and voting on such matters as the spending of tax money, the taking of land for public use, and the selection of judges and officers to run the town affairs. Originally the towns in Massachusetts were laid out in the style of an English "manor"—a style that was already out of fashion in England. Under this arrangement, the homes of the townspeople were all close together, and all near the meeting house, so they could walk there conveniently. The farm land, instead of being close to each house, was all laid out in fields outside the town. But each home, set on a single "main street," had a long "home lot" that might reach back for a mile and this by itself was sometimes enough to supply a small family with wood, garden, and pasture for its stock. When more was needed, each family was entitled to a strip of farm land in the field where all the others had their own strips. Effort was made to treat every townsman equally, so that there should be no aristocrats and so that ownership of land and property should never become more important than the Gospel and a righteous life. Pasturage for cattle was also supplied in a "common" where every townsman was entitled to let his cows or sheep roam. There was a town mill and town woods.

Because so much land was held in common, the townspeople had to share the work of keeping the land fenced. The town meeting would therefore elect "fence-viewers" (these are still elected in some small towns) to decide when repairs were needed as well as "field-drivers" to drive the cattle to and from the pasturage. Special bonuses were sometimes offered to bring in a miller to grind the town grain. There was one aspect of the manor system, however, that did not suit the people of Massachusetts, even though it was used in some of the other colonies. This was the system under which the lord of the manor, the wealthy man who held title to the land, would have control over the lives of all who lived and worked on his land, would be the judge, the mayor, and the military commander. He would "represent" all his tenants in the state legislature and even take upon himself the job of enforcing the laws.

In Massachusetts, it did not take long for newcomers to become infected with the love of democracy. In the beginning, many "freemen" even refused to observe some of the requests made by the king or some of the laws established for regulating trade in the colonies. Eventually, the original charter was withdrawn and for a time the colony lived under a dictatorial governor named Edmund Andros. Andros actually took away some of the lands that the colonists had bought from the Indians or claimed by right of settlement. A deed from an Indian, said Andros (and

The Great Seal of New England used during Edmond Andros's term of office

this remark was held against him for a long time), had no more value than the "scratch of a bear's claw." And no title was worth anything, in Andros's view, if it had not been granted or confirmed by the king or his official representative. At just about the time Parliament in England was inviting William of Orange to take the throne from King James, the Massachusetts colonists imprisoned Andros (his name was pronounced Andrews) and shipped him back to London. Then, under the new king, the colonists began to negotiate for a new charter.

Under the new charter, the vote was extended to all "free-holders"—men who owned a certain amount of property or had certain yearly income. This meant that members of churches other than the Congregational Church could now vote for representatives in the legislature (called the General Court) and could have a voice in town meetings. The governor was now to be appointed by the king and both governor and king could veto the acts of the legislature. In spite of these new restrictions, the habit of democracy spread still further and gradually the whole colony became addicted to running its own affairs. They even defied the governor in some matters and did not always obey the king when he tried to deprive them of certain rights they had been brought up to believe had always belonged to them.

The existence of the free schools meant that many more people could read and write. This set Massachusetts still further apart from other colonies by making it possible to spread the slogans of liberty far and wide and have them understood and supported.

But Massachusetts was different in physical ways too. The climate, that seemed so ideal to John Smith—not a single man of all his company fell sick here, he said—was harsher than that of England. The winter lasted longer; the cold froze more deeply; and the summer came with a sudden blast of heat. The colonists soon learned that good English wheat could not be raised on these shores. The sudden oncome of hot weather, after a long season of chilly nights, caused the wheat to grow ripe too suddenly, and to dry out on the stalk. So the colonists learned instead to depend on the Indian corn—or maize. This was really a grass that had been developed by Indian farmers over the centuries, until it grew its sweet seeds on large ears, some five or six to a stalk.

One thing that did grow exceedingly well in the long cool spring and in the warm days and dewy nights of summer was pasture grass. John Smith saw at once that cattle could be raised here easily and would feed themselves to fatness on the long lush grasses of the Massachusetts meadows. Early in the life of the colony, cows and sheep and pigs were brought over from the homeland. Sometimes, in a wild winter storm, they would have to be tossed overboard to lighten the ship and keep it from sinking. But enough of them were brought to shore safely so that before long the pastures were full of cattle. Beef became an important produce of Massachusetts, and much of it was sent back to England in trade. There were always cows to milk; and of course fences were needed to keep the cattle from wandering. The raising of cattle became so widespread that oxen rather than horses became the favorite beast of burden. Almost every farm in the province had one "yoke," or pair, of oxen that were used for plowing, for drawing the produce to market or the family to meeting, for pulling up the stumps of the many trees that had to be cut down, and for drawing aside the hundreds of enormous rocks that seemed to fill almost every field in the colony.

Everywhere you might look in Massachusetts, there were hills on the horizon—except of course if you stood on shore and looked right out to sea. It was difficult for a farmer to find anywhere more than ten acres that had no hill or

Oxen were used to transport families to Sunday meetings, as well as for farm chores

slope or gully. And hidden in all the hills, as John Smith had observed, was stone of every sort—gray granite with handsome veins in it; hard blue stone that a man might hammer all day before he could split it; sandstone that crumbled or split into slices under the plow; and large brooding boulders that looked as if they had been scattered helter skelter by a group of giants at play ten thousand years before.

The patient oxen would draw these stones together for the farmer, who then would pile them one on the other to make long low fences, just high enough to keep his cows or his sheep from straying. All over Massachusetts—indeed all over New England—those long stone fences still can be found, often hidden now in deep woods where there used to be a grassy clearing, reaching up hill and down hill and all along a roadside.

Poisonous snakes were very few in Massachusetts, mostly rock-rattlers in the western hills, and in Maine there were no poisonous snakes at all. But wolves were a danger to the Pilgrims while foxes and weasels and wolverines could destroy the farm animals and domestic fowl. In the very beginning, the Indians were no great threat to the settlers. Indeed, without them the settlers could not have survived, nor could the traders have found the rich supply of furs. The Indians at first did not really resent the white man's presence, except for a few of the more warlike tribes. The Indians never considered that any individual man could "own" the hills and the trees and the lakes and streams that God had laid down here for all to enjoy. They themselves were used to moving from place to place within their own tribal territory, to settle by a stream when the alewives (a fish like a herring) were running, for instance, or to erect their wigwams in wide clearings or on harbor islands to wait for the crops to ripen. They hunted freely all through the woodland, fished and dug clams and trapped lobsters wherever they pleased, and traded with the other tribes in the area.

The various Indian tribes throughout New England—Nipnets, Pequods, Narragansetts, and many others—usually dwelt in peace with each other, trading farm produce for furs, and sometimes paying visits to one another's home grounds. But occasionally there would be quarrels that developed into bloody warfare. One season, the Narragansett Indians, who dwelt along the shores of southern Massachusetts and Rhode Island, invited the Nipnets, who lived in mid-Massachusetts, to come visit them for a clam feast. The party was such a happy affair that the Nipnets invited the Narragansetts in turn to visit the Nipnet territory. The Nipnets were great fishermen. They had built weirs, or dams, in most of the big streams in their area, to trap fish and eels. When the Narragansetts came visiting, the Nipnets served their own specialty—eels roasted on hot coals. The Narragansetts were horrified. To them the eels were snakes and not fit for human fodder. They spit them out and fervently expressed their disgust. The Nipnets were enraged by this behavior and a bloody quarrel between the two tribes broke out, opening a breach between them that took a long time to heal.

The Indians were not a savage people. They lived by rules almost as rigid as those the Puritans set for themselves. Despite what white men liked to say about their "treachery," they had a high sense of honor. Said one English traveler about them: "They neither covet riches, nor dread poverty. They are Loyal to their Kings; Constant to their Wives; Indulgent to their Children; and Faithful to their Trust."

But the Indians did before long bitterly resent the white man's effort to extend his grasp of the land, to chop down the forests where the animals found cover, and to keep the Indians out of the fishing grounds that they had used off-and-on for hundreds of years. So fighting began between Indian and white man that lasted for many years and cost many lives. And because the distant king had dangers of his own to deal with, the Massachusetts colonists had to learn to defend themselves, not only against the perils of the forest and the weather, but against an armed and determined foe.

2 Fighting the Indians

Although the first colonists lived at peace with the Indians and in some instances even owed their lives to the friendly tribesmen who showed them how to grow corn and provide against the bitter winters, quarrels were inevitable. At first, the men who settled Massachusetts merely took over land left vacant when whole tribes of Indians had been wiped out by pestilence. But before long, they began to cut the timber off the Indians' hunting grounds and to try to keep the Indians out of fields where the tribes had roamed freely for centuries.

The first organized fighting took place along the Massachusetts coast between the Pequods and the white men. The whites, with the help of the Narragansetts and some other tribes, were soon victorious, and the war did not spread far through the colony. Indeed, just west of Boston, in the towns of Natick, Groton, Lowell, Littleton, Marlboro, Grafton, Hopkinton, and Canton, a gentle minister from England, John Eliot, established whole colonies of Indians who had been converted to Christianity. They were called the "praying Indians" and were often summoned to aid the English settlers against the other tribes.

By 1675, however, both Boston and Plymouth had grown into thriving prosperous towns and new settlers had built villages along the shore or farther inland along the wide Connecticut River. A brave young Indian decided to rally all the tribes to drive the white man off their land forever. This young man was named Metacomet. He was the son of a great chieftain, Massasoit, of the Wampanoag tribe, who had been a loyal friend of the first Plymouth colonists. The white men called Metacomet King Philip, although he was not really a king at all. He was, however, a fiery agitator and organizer who stirred the Indians to frenzy through his own boldness. King Philip personally visited many of the tribes throughout New England (his own territory was in Rhode Island) and inflamed their hatred of the white men by pointing out how the white men were pushing the Indians off their own land, setting cattle to graze in Indian cornfields, and putting fences around forest land that had once been open to all. Then Philip would stage a raid on some colonist's homestead, burning down the cabin, murdering the family, and stealing the cattle. The Indians, who had long been irritated by the white man's continued failure to keep his bargains and by the apparent impossibility of ever satisfying the desire of the white man for more and more land, were quick to follow Philip's example. Soon the whole colony was aflame and there was hardly a hamlet in all Massachusetts that did not live in dread of a sudden Indian attack. King Philip's bands rode everywhere throughout the colony, moving swiftly and silently, making no fires to betray their presence and always striking without warning. They might camp for days near some large town, awaiting the time when the colonists were least ready to fight, then riding in like madmen, to kill and burn and steal.

King Philip's followers of course could not keep all their doings secret, for there were still friendly Indians to bring word to the colonists that certain tribes were sharpening their tomahawks and tightening their bow strings. And the colonists had long been training themselves for war. Every household had its musket, its bullet molds, and its supply of flints. Every settlement had its public store of gunpowder. And the white men owned besides muskets and

Settlers would barricade their homes against sudden attack by bands of King Philip's followers

good horses, small cannon and armor. In open battle, the Indians could never stand against the whites and many of the red men were frightened of their gunpowder and overawed by their appearance. There was a story at this time of a horde of Indians who ran away from battle when they saw a white man take off his wig and put it in his pocket before raising his musket. Seeing a man with "two heads" was, according to the tale, more than the Indians could stand.

Some white men at this time used to speak scornfully of the Indians as being given to fighting from ambush and being "too cowardly" to engage in open battle. And this is exactly what the British soldiers would say about the American soldiers a hundred years later.

The tribes that fought for King Philip were not cowards. They knew how to take advantage of concealment offered by the woods and swamps, and they were expert at creeping close to a white settlement undetected. They could not be frightened away by guns or by the white man's magic. They were ready to die to help rid the land of these creatures who were robbing them of their farms and hunting grounds. And they were scornful of the "praying Indians" and forced many of them, by threats and violence, to abandon the towns the white men had given them.

Altogether, King Philip's forces killed more than six hundred settlers, in battle or by massacre. They fell upon some thirteen towns in Massachusetts, Plymouth Colony, and Rhode Island, killed many of the people, burned their houses, and stuck the bodies of victims on poles as an example to the rest. The settlers fought back valiantly and often, through sheer daring, managed to hold the Indians at bay until help arrived. But while King Philip lived, the Indians remained on the warpath and white men slept uneasily at night. Eventually, in August 1676, a renegade Indian found Philip in the Wampanoag stronghold at Mount Hope, Rhode Island, and murdered him. Without his leadership, the Indian alliance collapsed and the white man captured and executed many of them—some of them on mere suspicion of having helped King Philip.

For a long time after that Indians were not permitted to enter Boston without a guard "and two Musketeers," and they were never allowed to stay overnight. The large towns thereafter were free of Indian attack but the small villages along the frontier—in Maine—were in constant danger from the natives, who might be friendly one day and ready to make war the next. It was in these areas that the settlers were reaching out to take hold of more land. Judge Samuel Sewall, a leading magistrate in the province, sternly warned that if the colonists did not set aside some lands that would belong to the Indians, the Indians were not likely to believe that the Christians would grant them room in Heaven either. But a farmer always needs a little more land if his farm is thriving. He needs a new woodlot, to provide fuel for future winters, or extra pasture to feed more cattle, or room on which a newly married son can build a house for himself. And so the frontier farmers kept clearing and fencing off more and more of the free wilderness.

The men in the small villages were jealous of the French hold on the fisheries and trading posts, off the coasts of Maine and of Acadia (the old-time name for Nova Scotia). They kept trying to push the boundary of the British lands farther and farther to the east. The French, for their part, desired to take over all the lands in New England and keep the fisheries for themselves. To help them accomplish this, and to fight off the English efforts to add French lands to their own, the French made frequent use of the Indians.

The religion of the French gave the English colonists a special reason to hate and fear them. All Papists (that is, Roman Catholics) were completely outside the true religion, the Puritans felt, and they would not even grant that Papists could be Christians. The French, meanwhile, used their own missionaries to encourage the Indians to drive out the English. As a result there were frequent raids on the villages and small forts that lay along the edges of the English territory. Sometimes the Indians would kill one or two of the colonists whom they happened to catch in the open—on their way to work in the fields, on the way to meeting, on the way to market. It was a foolish colonist who made such journeys without his musket in hand. But sometimes, as when working in the fields, it was simply impossible to keep a gun in one hand. Then the men and boys might take care never to work near the edge of the field, where a lean, naked brown arm might reach up out of the brush and silently yank a white man over the stone fence to his death.

The Indians did not kill all their captives by any means. Often they took the strong young men, the children, and the women back to Canada, or kept them in the Indian villages, to be slaves, or turned them over to missionaries to be converted to Catholicism. Many a young girl was raised in a Canadian convent after being taken captive by Indians. And sometimes she lost all desire to return to her old life or even to see her family again. Sometimes the women might marry Indians and live as members of the tribe. Most often, however, the whites were enslaved and lived lives of unceasing labor, frequent physical punishment, and loneliness. But even some of the boys learned to become good Indians, spoke the language, adopted the Indian dress, and become active members of the tribe. From time to time, captives were recovered, or escaped, or were ransomed in some way, occasionally returning after many years.

Once during a peace parley between the military leaders of Massachusetts Bay and some Indians, the white men asked that the Indians return, as part of the price of peace, a boy named Macfarlane, who had been taken captive a few years earlier. The Indians agreed to bring the boy to the next meeting. But when the meeting was held, the boy was not produced and the colonists found themselves surrounded by none but feathered Indians. The spokesman for the colonists was indignant when the boy did not appear and he warned the Indian chief that this could mean the end of the truce. The chief apologized and promised that he would bring the boy with him to the very *next* meeting. That would not do, the white man shouted, and his companions all added their own angry voices. But the Indians sat silent and expressionless. Finally, after the white men had spent nearly all their rage, an old sachem stood up and took the hand of a strong and well-clothed young brave. He led him into the center of the circle.

"Here is your Macfarlane," he said.

The young brave solemnly greeted the white man in the Indian tongue. But this merely heightened the white leader's anger. This, he warned the sachem furiously, is no time for jokes.

"But I am Macfarlane," said the young man, in perfect English. The white men stared openmouthed. It was indeed Macfarlane, bronzed from going hatless in the sun, as white men never did, and dressed in buckskin like a brave. The Indians howled with laughter at the success of their joke. And they parted sorrowfully with their young brave, who was learned now in Indian ways and Indian language and was as straight and strong as any of them.

Captivity did not often end as happily as this and killings were all too frequent. Horses and cattle were stolen, houses robbed and burned, and sometimes whole families driven into the forests or forced to take refuge on some island off the shore. The records of the years in the late 1600's and early 1700's are full of sad tales of men and women murdered in the fields, or while walking the roads, or even slaughtered in their homes. But the Indians too had tales to tell of armed white men who destroyed their encampments, killed and scalped the men, women, and children, and drove the Indians away from their hunting and fishing grounds. The French authorities often paid the Indians bounties, or rewards, in French crowns, for each English scalp turned in, or for every captive. But the English with their own Indian allies, the Mohawks and Iroquois, served the same sort of medicine to the French, and no one can say just which side began it. It is certain however that for many years—almost to the time of the Revolution—some of the colonial governments were paying bounties for Indian scalps, without asking how or why the Indians were killed. Indians, to many of the frontier men, were no more than animals, to be exterminated without mercy, so they would not exist to annoy the white man or hunt on the land the white man wanted for his own.

It is certain that the king of England offered the frontier folk of Massachusetts very small protection from Indian raids. What arms they used against the Indians were chiefly of their own providing. But Massachusetts was important to England, especially because it supplied such excellent timber for masts, spars, and planking. (In Maine the great pines and spruces would reach sixty, seventy, even a hundred feet into the sky, taller than two telephone poles, and straight as a shaft of light.) Consequently, the people of the province felt they were justified in begging their king to send them help in the long long war with the Indians and French. They needed food and they especially needed ships and soldiers.

The British had many other battles to fight, however, in other parts of the world. There was a rebellion in Ireland and a war with France and with Portugal that took all the force the king could spare. To the aid of Massachusetts, the British Crown sent two warships—too big to fight in coastal waters—and a succession of poorly trained military leaders, who could not conceal their contempt for the colonists and who knew nothing whatever about fighting the Indians.

Beginning in 1688 and continuing for nearly thirty years, with a few brief truces and some peace treaties that were soon broken, the men of Massachusetts—with the frequent assistance of fighters from Plymouth Colony, from Connecticut, and New Hampshire—fought off the Indians and French. Every small village along the frontier had its blockhouse, to which the farmers and village folk would retreat when scouts brought news of the approach of Indians. And the Indian raids were frequent, until they seemed no more unusual than thunderstorms. Every family in the frontier country—in Maine, New Hampshire, and western Massachusetts—had members who had been killed or carried away, and every village had its own story of a gallant fight against Indian raiders, or of a night and day expedition into the deep wilderness to overtake some Indian raiding party and recover its captives. While there were plenty of brave men and women throughout the frontier land to help fight off the Indians or to follow them into the woods and force them to yield up their booty, it was extremely difficult to maintain an army. The province was too poor to pay its soldiers in anything but paper money, which sometimes proved to be not worth as much as it was supposed to be. And the temptation to wander off, or to settle down in idleness somewhere, or even to make a few sharp trades with the Indians—who always had excellent furs to offer—was sometimes too much for the soldiers. Also there seemed no real end to the fighting. The Indian was such an elusive foe, and the Canadian French were so well supplied and so quick to return raid for raid, that hardly any headway was made.

At one point a brave, plainspoken, hearty man from Maine—Sir William Phips—organized and led an expedition against the city of Port Royal in Acadia (it is now Annapolis, Nova Scotia). He scored a quick and complete victory and returned in triumph to Boston after having exacted from the Acadians an oath of allegiance to the king of England. The Massachusetts people rejoiced at the ap-

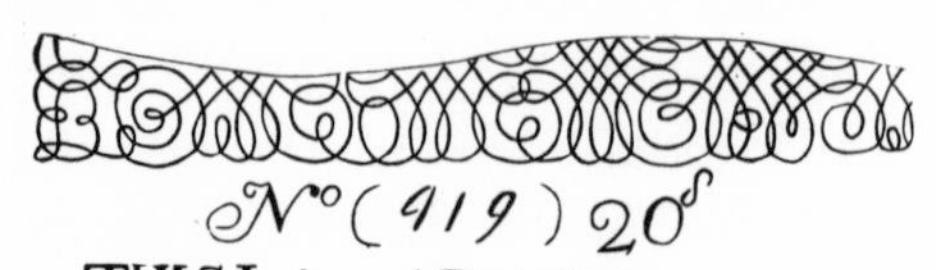

No (919) 20s

THIS Indented Bill of Twenty Shillings due from the Maſſachuſets Colony to the Poſſeſſor ſhall be in value equal to money & ſhall be accordingly accepted by the Treaſurer and Receivers ſubordinate to him in all Publick paym.ts and for any Stock at any time in the Treaſury. Boston in New-England February the third 1690 By Order of the General Court

Elisha Hutchinson
John Phillips
Tim Thornton
Comitee

A facsimile of the first paper money used in New England

parent wiping out of this stronghold that had sent so many ships out to capture and destroy their fishing vessels. But the next time a French warship sailed into Port Royal, the Acadians reversed their pledge of allegiance and the raids on the fishermen's vessels were resumed.

The Massachusetts leader tried hard to persuade the traders in Albany to help them get the Iroquois and the Mohawks (who had been converted by Protestant missionaries) to aid the colonists against the Abnaki Indians of the east. But the traders were far more interested in trade and saw no reason for sacrificing it in order to protect the frontiers of Massachusetts.

But trade was one of the weapons that the Massachusetts men used too. The Indians always found it easier and more profitable to trade with the Englishmen—except when they dealt with some of the scoundrels who would cheat them or steal their goods. So they would halt the fighting every now and then to resume the profitable trade. But then the French would send a new and more belligerent leader who would rally the Abnaki to strike the Englishmen more fiercely than ever. The Iroquois Indians sometimes helped by sending word of an impending raid, but the colonists did not always believe them. They sometimes became almost indifferent to such warnings, as people who live on the side of a volcano may learn to ignore the rumblings and occasional explosions from within the mountain. Because a warning was ignored, the residents of Deerfield, Massachusetts, were slaughtered and the town laid waste. And the citizens of Massachusetts Bay were once more aroused to strike a heavy blow against Canada. They insisted to the king that until Canada was taken entirely out of French hands, there would be no peace in Massachusetts. The province had lost many of its frontier villages—even Falmouth (now Portland), Maine, and some of its largest forts had been destroyed.

But Massachusetts, when it had leaders who knew how to conduct a war—and how to win the aid of neighboring colonies—eventually found ways of defeating the Indians. One method that seemed to work miraculously was evolved by a native of Massachusetts, Governor Joseph Dudley, who put his soldiers on snowshoes so they could attack the Indian villages during the depth of winter. By the use of snowshoes, a soldier carrying a heavy pack and musket would still move swiftly over the surface of snow that was five feet deep. And in the woods along the Maine and New Hampshire frontiers, the winter snows often reached this depth. The Indians, camped snugly in their wigwams along the rivers, with the rising smoke betraying the location of their village to a watcher miles away, never expected to see English soldiers coming in over the breast-deep snow. And so the Abnaki were often taken unawares and defeated.

But whenever the Massachusetts men had won what seemed like a permanent victory on the frontier, the home government would make peace with France on terms that were a deep disappointment to the colonists. In 1698, the English signed a treaty that gave Acadia back to France, even though the people of Massachusetts felt that it belonged to them by right of conquest—and despite fears in Massachusetts that the French would once more begin to raid the fishing and trading vessels from the colony. The Abnaki Indians, meanwhile, kept on fighting, with the secret encouragement of the French.

In 1713, after another war that had begun in 1702, the French and British signed a new treaty, this time giving Acadia over to English control along with Newfoundland. But the French insisted this did not include Cape Breton Island, which the colonists had always considered a part of Acadia. And on Cape Breton the French promptly built the fortress of Louisbourg, many times stronger than Port Royal had been and so a far greater threat to the ships from Boston.

The Indians, as before, continued to fight, even though they had now twice acknowledged that they were subjects of the English king. And, as before, the French authorities continued to supply and secretly encourage the Indians. Meanwhile, the colonists of Massachusetts began to push the Indians farther back from the coast and up the Maine rivers, so that white men could cut the rich timber, clear land for farming, and fence off pasture for cattle. And once more the private traders undertook to cheat the Indians in every way possible, so that the Abnaki, weary as they were from the years of fighting, still grew angry enough to kill. It was hard for an Indian to understand why he should accept as "legal" a piece of paper giving title to the land to some white man, when the paper had not been signed by

An Indian deed confirming the title of Boston Peninsula. Indians and settlers alike often disregarded such documents when they interfered with the free use of hunting grounds or farm lands

the Indian himself but by his grandfather—and most likely by a drunken grandfather at that. He insisted the land was still his to hunt and camp on and he refused to live in peace with the men who drove him away from it.

The Abnaki crept out at night to slaughter the cattle of the settlers on the Maine frontiers, and the Indians on Cape Sable took their canoes to sea to capture fishing vessels and other ships from the colony. But now the colonists had learned some lessons from the many years of fighting. They hired scouting parties to move from town to town to keep track of where the Indians were and what they were planning. They organized surprise attacks on Indian settlements. And they set a high reward for Indian scalps, which tempted hundreds of men to volunteer to go out into the woods to hunt the Indians down. All over the state, men formed companies to go scalphunting, and the slaughter

The coast of Maine provided fishing grounds, farm land, and an ample supply of lumber for new settlers

among the Indians was horrible. So high was the bounty set on scalps that the General Court at one point had to order the treasurer of the colony to bury all the scalps that had been turned in to him. Young men had begun to steal the scalps back and turn them in again and again to collect new rewards.

With the Indians finally subdued, the colonists showed that they had also learned how to keep peace. They forbade private traders to deal with the Indians any longer. Instead the government of Massachusetts set up public storehouses all along the frontier, where Indians could sell their furs at good prices, without danger of being cheated or robbed. New settlers flocked to the wild lands of Maine to build new villages, each with its blockhouse fort, and to clear away more and more of the forests where the Abnaki warriors had for so long made their hiding places.

3 The Witches

Like many who have been brought up to believe that only members of their own church will enjoy the blessings of Heaven, the Puritans of Massachusetts were impatient with any who refused to embrace their church, or denied the truth of its doctrines. And they could be extremely cruel to those who preached or subscribed to "heresy"—that is, a teaching not accepted by their church.

All those who first came to Massachusetts followed the same faith—that form of Protestant Christianity first preached in England by John Calvin. The men and women who founded Boston and the other towns outside the original Plymouth Colony were even more strict in their devotion to Calvin's teachings than were the Pilgrims. Calvin had taught them that only membership in the Church Militant (by which he meant a Congregational Church) would assure men and women of a place in Heaven. Membership in a church meant living by a strict set of rules that were intended to keep people's minds centered on hard work, meditation, and prayer. The Puritans did not believe in a Universal or National Church. Each of their "churches" was a group of people (a congregation) who made their own "covenant with God." Puritanism had actually started in England about 1550 when certain of the clergy in the Established Church of England refused to wear heavily decorated robes. And it was by their simple black clothing as much as by their long faces and solemn expressions that the New England Puritans could be known.

John Calvin would not even permit the use of harmony—a blending of voices for a pleasant effect—in the singing of psalms. All was simple. All was somber. All was strictly in accordance with the rules.

From the very beginning, there were some who did not devote themselves to the Puritan way of life with as much enthusiasm as they might have. These men and women sometimes found themselves barred from full membership in the church—and thus unable to vote in provincial elections—and until they did proper penance and corrected their ways, they could not be married in the church, nor could they take communion, nor have their children baptized by the minister.

But there were some, even among those who were high in their church, and who were considered devout members, who found these harsh practices altogether out of tune with Christianity. Some dared to disagree openly with the ministers and because of their disagreement received punish-

Those who did not properly devote themselves to the Puritan way of life were often publicly punished

ments so harsh that it is hard to believe religious people could have approved of them. But the Puritans, like some other peoples who have made a show of their own righteousness, told themselves that the more harshly they punished the teachers of heresy, the harder they were fighting for the victory of the true religion.

One of the very first to feel the wrath of the Puritan elders was an intelligent, witty, sweet-natured, and well-educated lady, the daughter of a clergyman, who came to Boston when the town was still brand new, and Massachusetts was under its first governor, John Winthrop. Her name was Anne Hutchinson. She and her husband had come to Boston from their comfortable home in Lincolnshire, in England, to follow the pastor they were devoted to —John Cotton, minister of St. Botolph's Church (from which the name Boston—"Botolph's Town"—was taken). Cotton himself fled to New England to escape the anger of the bishops of the church, who were intent on punishing all Puritans. Anne Hutchinson in Boston, as she had done at home in England, enjoyed John Cotton's sermons so much that she liked to invite other ladies into her home after services to talk about the sermons. As a girl in the home of her father, the Reverend Francis Marbury, she had been free to engage in religious discussions, although most women of that day had very little education and were not encouraged to study or to take part in learned conversations. But Anne could express herself with wit and with clarity and people enjoyed listening to her. As a result, her parlor was often crowded on Sunday by ladies in their hoods, and sometimes gentlemen would even gather at the open doors and windows and pay attention to what she said.

Before long she began to express ideas that were not strictly in line with the teachings of Calvin. Calvin held that men and women were "elected" to the true church to begin with and then, by careful obedience and strict attention to religious duties, they could attain full membership, not just in the living church but in the Church Triumphant on Judgment Day. Those who did not follow this route, which was laid out as plainly as lines on a map, would suffer eternal punishment. But Mrs. Hutchinson argued, from her own meditations, that direct communication with God was like the sudden hearing of an inner voice, which might come even to those who had not followed the path so carefully laid down.

Such a teaching had the effect, the Puritan ministers saw, of making God's grace "free"—so that almost anyone might reach Heaven. It also had the effect of making it difficult to tell saint from sinner, because if a man who did not always wear black clothes and hat and did not quote the Bible and respect the clergy could still get to Heaven—then how could you tell when a man was "being good"? And the Puritan ministers—after a two-day trial, during which poor Anne Hutchinson was forced to stand on her feet and be questioned without a moment's rest—declared Anne Hutchinson "unfit for our society," and she was ordered to leave the colony. She took refuge in Rhode Island, where she lived like a hunted person for a time and was finally slain by Indians. Her grandson, by a strange quirk of fate, came to be Governor of Massachusetts. And her teachings were taken up eventually by the Quakers, who were also considered unfit to live in Massachusetts.

One Quaker, Mary Dyer, who had been banished from Massachusetts Bay as a disciple of Anne Hutchinson, was hanged on Boston Common in 1660 after she had refused to stay away. Other Quakers were punished in the same manner, and one citizen of Boston who took pity on Quakers who had been thrown in jail without food or blankets was himself ordered out of the province. Anabaptists, who believed that boys and girls should not be baptized until they were grown up, were persecuted in similar manner.

Even the Puritan leaders, many of whom were kind men in every other way—John Winthrop, who took time in the rush of starting his voyage to the new world to send Valentine's greetings to his beloved wife, and John Cotton, whose gentleness and apparent broadmindedness had won the profound admiration of Anne Hutchinson herself—themselves approved of and actively promoted these cruelties. For they were sincerely convinced that God wanted them to treat His enemies in this manner.

One governor of Massachusetts who did not approve of the banishment was Sir Harry Vane—a handsome, courageous, and brilliant young man of twenty-four, heir to a fine fortune, who had given up an assured future in England to join the New England Puritans. Sir Harry was chosen governor of the colony just a year after he landed in Boston and he proved an able and level-headed administrator. He was shrewd and tactful in dealing with the Indians. He was respectful and thoughtful in working with men older than himself. But he came quickly under the influence of the lively Mrs. Hutchinson and adopted her point of view. He had opposed the clergy at home and he was not afraid to do the same here, in the name of religious liberty. He was especially opposed to a new law that laid a penalty on anyone who, without obtaining special permission, received into his household a stranger who came into the province with the intention of staying. Because of his opposition to this measure, which was intended to keep supporters of Mrs. Hutchinson from moving into Massachusetts, Vane fell out of favor and Winthrop was named governor again. But Harry Vane left with a good word for the man who had replaced him and remained a friend of Massachusetts all his life.

The Puritan elders thus worked all the time to keep the

peace and quiet of their little domain from being disturbed, and they remained quick to drive out or turn away those who held strange beliefs. They also, after a time, began to look suspiciously at any who might be guilty of making agreements with the Powers of Darkness.

Having no knowledge of natural laws, the church elders of that day explained almost all the workings of nature as acts of God or of the Devil, depending on whether or not they seemed in accordance with God's rules. While God might send a thunderstorm or a contrary wind to warn, or to punish his elected ones, or even to keep them from falling into harm's way, it was the Devil who made animals or growing grain or the silent earth behave in some outlandish fashion, or who gave strange powers to men and women. Sudden seizures, pains, and afflictions, or odd noises in the head, or dishes that broke without apparent cause could be blamed on the Devil or upon those who did his work. Insane people or those who had fits or who saw visions were all thought to be in the grip of evil spirits or actually communicating with the Prince of Darkness.

Witches—who could be either men or women—had long been persecuted in Old England. When James VI of Scotland came to the British throne, he made a special task of ridding his kingdom of people who were in league with the Devil. This was in 1603, seventeen years before the Pilgrims set sail to New England. King James had written a book called *Demonology,* which was a study of witchcraft, and he ordered a new law enacted to make witchcraft a crime punishable by death.

The Puritans in Old England hunted witches most eagerly. And they continued to do so in New England even after the practice died out in the homeland. That was largely because the Puritans' strict control over learning made it difficult for people to share the gradual growth of scientific knowledge. It was also true that the Puritan religion had a fiercer quality and that its ministers were more used to judging individuals harshly and punishing them severely. They were also more deeply involved, in their own minds, in a day-to-day struggle with their Unseen Enemy. Witches were believed in by other religions and persecuted, even executed by them. But no Puritan judge in that day would ever have taken the easy-going attitude of William Penn in Pennsylvania who acquitted a confessed witch in 1684. Even though the poor old lady "admitted" that she had flown through the air on a broomstick, William Penn let her go on the ground that there was no law against traveling about in that fashion.

Long before the dreadful trials in Salem that led to the hanging of nineteen witches and the death of another by "pressing," there had been trials in Massachusetts of men and women who were accused of being in communication with the Devil. The law in Massachusetts ordered that any person who "hath or consulteth with a familiar spirit" should be put to death. A "familiar spirit" could only be a messenger from the Devil's domain. Under this law, Anne

So-called witches were hunted out and placed under arrest in New England long before the infamous Salem trials took place

Hibbins was put to death in Boston in 1656. She was the wife of William Hibbins, a near neighbor of Governor Winthrop, and formerly official agent of the province in London. She was a refined and highly moral lady. But she was unable to prove herself innocent. Several other accused witches were able to establish their innocence and so were acquitted. But most of them discovered that if they said their accusers were lying, or if they protested their arrest too strongly, they only made themselves look more guilty than ever, for their judges would argue that only an agent of the Devil would dare assail the authorities in that manner.

In 1688, Cotton Mather, son of Increase Mather, and a descendant of John Cotton himself, became directly involved in a case of witchcraft. Mather was unquestionably the most influential minister of his day—an educated and, for his time, broadminded man who spoke up for religious tolerance when the Puritans were eager to return to their original system of government-by-the-True-Church-only. But on the subject of witchcraft Mather had a closed mind. Witches were not human beings in his eyes. They were the living body of the Ancient Enemy, the Devil. Great authorities everywhere for more than a century had known of their existence, and had warned of their sly, magical, and daring efforts to force good people into Sin and win the world away from God. Therefore he felt it his holy duty to stand up to them and wipe them off the face of the earth. A man named John Goodwin, a good church member with four children, complained to Mather that his thirteen-year-old daughter had been so severely scolded by a neighbor that the girl began to have fits. The fits, which were probably hysterical, were described as "of a diabolical character"—that is, the result of the Devil's influence. Her screaming and crying soon frightened her sister and two brothers into the same state, so that all four little bodies seemed to have been taken over by a quartet of evil spirits. And the hot-tempered neighbor, Mrs. Glover, was thereupon deemed a witch.

The Reverend Cotton Mather, feeling that he might, by his religious powers, be able to exorcise or drive out the spirits, took the eldest, Martha, into his home. But the solemn incantations of the holy man seemed merely to drive the poor girl to newer and wilder performances. Thereupon Mrs. Glover was arrested and in her house the investigators found "puppets" or dolls that were accepted as evidence that she had been creating unholy images of some sort. When Cotton Mather endeavored to pray with her to help drive off the Devil, Mrs. Glover, an Irish Catholic, refused to join him without the consent of "a good Catholic spirit." Cotton Mather assumed that she meant that she must have the consent of the Devil. This was enough to convict her and the poor lady was hanged.

But the trials that really disgraced the province and that won for Salem, Massachusetts, the name of "Witch City" took place in 1692. These trials, like that of Mrs. Glover, were prompted by the hysterical acts of children who were believed to have come under the influence of a witch. Actually they came under the influence of a West Indian woman who was a slave in the household of the Reverend Samuel Parris of Salem Village (now called Danvers). The slave was named Tituba, and she was the wife of Indian John. She was skilled in the tricks and illusions and mysterious practices that we know as "voodoo," and she enjoyed showing them to a group of young girls—ages nine to twenty—who gathered at the minister's house from time to time. The girls were quick to learn and to practice the tricks, which included going into a sort of trance in which the body would twist and contort and give out strange sounds. The girls' parents in alarm sought the help of the local physician who, when he could find no other name for the ailment, called it witchcraft. The children, frightened now, and undoubtedly thinking that they themselves might be taken for witches and cruelly punished, were quick to point out the people who they believed had wished these seizures on them. They named Tituba of course and two poor bedraggled women of the town who at least had the appearance of witches.

The children were not trying to be vicious. They were scared and excited by the solemnity with which they were examined by the grim-faced men in black clothes. And they were eager as well to avoid being accused of wickedness themselves, and so they hastened to give "evidence" against the poor women who had been arrested. And Tituba, quick to see how she might save her own life, hastened to "confess" that she had been in league with the Devil, and accused the other two women of having also been in communication with the Powers of Darkness. But she went even further. With very little urging she named as witches two highly respected housewives of the town. The girls, and the mother of one of the girls, added further "evidence" against these ladies—one of whom had been on unfriendly terms with the family of the girl who acted as chief accuser.

The naming of two respected ladies as dealers in Black Magic put the whole village into an uproar and filled many families with terror, especially those who had ever said or done anything to make enemies of the "afflicted" girls or their families. When a local minister (not Mr. Parris) preached a fiery sermon against witches, his talk was interrupted by cries and contortions on the part of the frightened girls, who had probably by this time begun to take a strange pleasure in being the "heroines" of the episode.

Two of the girls who had been servants in the home of John Proctor accused him of being a witch and he was promptly locked in jail. A man named George Jacobs was accused by his grand-daughter of having helped her become

Frightened people hastened to save themselves from charges of witchcraft by giving evidence against their neighbors

a witch. After that, "confessions" and accusations followed one upon the other, as frightened people hastened to save themselves by "giving evidence" against their neighbors. And the accused were placed in the position of having to prove their innocence. It was impossible for them to do so, for much of the evidence against them was "spectral" evidence—that is, stories of visions and dreams the girls had seen. An accused person was faced with the bitter choice of calling the accusations lies (which was just what a witch *would* do, according to the judges) or of saving his own life by confessing his guilt and naming somebody else as a fellow-witch.

The easiest person to give evidence against, in making a confession of this sort, was somebody who had already been accused by others. So the arrested people were often faced with testimony from several different sources. One poor woman, the mother of four small girls, faced the horror of seeing her little eight-year-old, scared out of her own wits, taking the stand to testify that her mother had made her a witch when she was six. On the testimony of this terrified child, the mother was put to death and Cotton Mather openly gloried in her execution. "This rampant hag," he called her, although she had lived a life of hard work and devotion. And he dwelt on the fact that her accusers had "confessed" that the Devil had told them he was going to make her Queen of Hell. The poor tortured woman, whose name was Martha Carrier, was finally driven to exclaim to the magistrates: "It is a shameful thing that you should mind these folks who are out of their wits!" They were all liars, she insisted. But this was obvious "witch-talk" to the magistrates, and Mrs. Carrier had now condemned herself past saving.

Altogether that summer, between June 19 and September 22, thirteen women and seven men were executed. On the final day, eight people were hanged at the same time, before a noisy crowd, including many who had given false evidence against them. The trials that convicted these people were not trials so much as investigations. The accused stood surrounded by hostile witnesses, hostile spectators, and hostile magistrates. She (or he) was not allowed a lawyer. The magistrates took turns in quizzing the accused, asking questions designed to trap them into damaging admissions. The accused could not question his accusers. He was forced to stand between judges and the accusers, whereupon the judges would ask, "Why did you afflict these children?" The accused of course could not answer such a question except to deny that he had afflicted anyone. Often at this point, the accuser, who might be one of the children, or Tituba's husband Indian John, would fall on the floor and roll around in an apparent seizure. The accused would be ordered to keep his eyes off the "victim" but to place his hands on her (or him). If the accused would not do this, officers of the court would seize him and force him to lay a hand on the victim. Thereupon the victim would suddenly be "cured." This was considered evidence enough of guilt and unless the accused promptly confessed that he was in league with the Devil and named his co-witches, he would be certain to be condemned to death.

Sometimes one of the supposed "victims" might approach the accused before the trial and ask his or her name. Then, when the "seizure" took place, the accuser would cry out this name and beg to be relieved of the affliction. The proceedings were almost too crude to be believed, and of course we tell ourselves today that we would never allow ourselves to be persuaded by such means.

But if we try to imagine how we might behave if all the "respectable" people we knew believed that evil deeds and strange happenings were ordered by the Devil, who worked through secret agents living right among us, it is easier to understand how normal people could be persuaded to hate accused "witches." Often, in our own lives, we have seen how people can be made to look guilty through newspaper stories and broadcasts, until anyone who stands up for them is suspected of being guilty of the same crime. And sometimes we even honor judges for treating accused people with great severity, forgetting that judges are to be honored for being fairminded and for guarding the rights of the accused as well as those of the accuser.

Cotton Mather was not a judge at the Salem trials but he did approve of their purpose—that is, the ferreting out and destruction of agents of the Devil. The methods used at Salem, however, were never approved by Mather. He decried the use of confessed witches as witnesses against honorable citizens. The witches were in league with the Devil he said and were not to be believed. He strongly disapproved of the use of the visions of the victims as evidence. The

Devil, said Mather, could very easily disguise himself as an innocent person and so delude these victims into blaming some innocent for their affliction. If witches were to be convicted, said he, they must be convicted by human evidence, just as accused people were convicted of other crimes. Mather did approve of the conviction of some of the accused, particularly of poor George Burroughs, whom the crowd almost saved from execution because he impressed the onlookers by his calmness in repeating the Lord's Prayer. Mather affirmed that he himself would have found Burroughs guilty, because he had been convicted on "proper" evidence.

There were, of course, people who protested the trials and executions despite the danger that they might themselves be accused. One of the magistrates, Nathaniel Saltonstall, walked out of the trials after the first woman had been found guilty. He was, he said, very much dissatisfied with the proceedings. But there were far more influential men to press for more and more convictions. And many people found a fierce satisfaction in identifying and exposing the enemy and in scoring such complete victories over the Devil—whom the Bible taught them to fear, to fight, and to destroy.

Cotton Mather has been largely blamed for stirring up the people of the colony against witches and so contributing to the madness at Salem. But Mather's chief part at Salem was to console the accused and try to win them back through repentance and confession. He was not a vindictive man nor a cruel one. For his time he was exceptionally tolerant. He believed in the Devil as sincerely as other men believe in God and was ready to fight Satan, and all his agents, with every weapon he owned, and chiefly by righteousness, fasting, and prayer. He approved of the execution of guilty witches. But he protested against the failure of the Salem judges to protect the rights of the accused. It was the preaching of less learned and more vindictive men that kept the populace in a rage.

But eventually there were too many killings. The sight of eight of their neighbors—good gentle people exactly like themselves—all hanging on the gallows together saddened the watchers and made some of them stop and think. What had these poor people actually done that could be proved against them? Was it right to accept as evidence the "visions" and the "spirit voices" that frightened children reported? Was it fair to range the whole town against them and not even allow them a lawyer to advise them and examine the witnesses? Was it right to force them to give testimony and then condemn them because they refused to answer or did not answer properly? Such questions began to trouble the more thoughtful people throughout the province even while the most ardent witch-hunters, like the Reverend Mr. Parris, in whose household the first witch was found, rejoiced at the killings and called for more.

As for the children, whom history has blamed for much of the cruelty and injustice, they were just children. They had been brought up in fear of witches. They were told by their own parents and ministers that they had been bewitched, and they had been taught to accept such decisions by their elders. They were in deadly fear that they might themselves be tortured and killed. And mixed with this fear must have been a terrible burden of guilt, so they dared not admit even to themselves that they had not told the solemn truth. Their visions could have been very real, the product of hysteria induced by intense fear and excitement. And surely it was their elders, and not they, who put the ropes around the necks of the innocents. It is worth remembering too that even the victims, although never doubting their own innocence, sincerely believed, as all their neighbors did, that there were such things as witches, and that they should be caught and punished. Mary Easty, one of the ladies who was hanged, wrote from her jail cell a letter that contained this sentence: "The Lord in His infinite mercy direct you in this great work if it be His blessed will that no more innocent blood be shed."

Mary Easty's voice was not heard however. What happened was that the witch-hunt began to reach rather too far, until it approached the very households of Cotton Mather and of the governor himself, William Phips, who had been away from Massachusetts during the trials. In October someone gave evidence against the wife of the Reverend John Hale of Beverly, who had himself been active in the witch-hunts. Governor Phips's wife was also accused as was the Reverend Samuel Willard, pastor of Boston's Old South Church, and it was whispered that there was a witch in Cotton Mather's family. Governor Phips, a man not much given to deep and involved thinking on religious matters, had never been enthusiastic about the witch trials. Now he ordered the Salem Court dissolved. It was becoming very clear to the people in power how difficult it was to defend an innocent person against the accusation when denial was taken as proof of guilt. They could tolerate such doings only when plain people were involved. But when it began to reach into the seat of government, it had gone far enough.

In May 1693, Governor Phips ordered the release of all those—and there were more than a hundred of them—who still sat in jail awaiting trial on a charge of witchcraft. But there was one important investigation still to come. This started in September 1693 when a Boston woman named Margaret Rule began to have fits that seemed "diabolical." She blamed them on a neighbor woman. Her story was that she was visited by specters, or ghosts, who asked her to sign a book they carried. It was, of course, "the Devil's Book." When she refused to sign it she said she was suddenly afflicted by strange ailments that forced her to stay in bed for six weeks. Then the "master specter" appeared. He was a "short, black man" who ordered that she be tortured. And tortured she was, by the pinching of invisible fingers and the pricking of invisible pins.

At this point she came under the observation of Cotton Mather, who remarked on the unhappy condition of her family and decided to do what he could to help her. He noted that she could, when under this spell, go without food for days without losing weight or feeling hunger. The specters, she said, forced her to drink a strange drink that made changes in her skin as if she had been dusted by powder and burned by sulphur, which raised blisters that quickly disappeared.

Mather, who prided himself on his learning, insisted that there was no disease known that could create such symptoms and so she was clearly afflicted by some agent of the Devil. Under the observation of Cotton Mather and his famous father, Increase Mather, poor Margaret began to develop all sorts of odd symptoms. She felt herself being lifted into the air. She heard strange noises in the room. She felt an animal like a rat brushing against her, an animal that could not be cornered. And she had visions of the future. Both Cotton Mather and his father tried by prayer, incantation, and the "laying on of hands" to chase the specters away, while the poor woman moaned and described her visions to the people who stood around her.

Finally, said Margaret, a "white spirit" came into view who persuaded the chief demon to drive all the black specters out of the room. After that Margaret, left limp and almost speechless, began to recover. It had taken six weeks for the seizure to leave her, and during this time a great many people had come to look at her and to watch the Mathers at their work and to marvel at the doings of the dark spirits.

This case seemed to strengthen the movement against

witchcraft, as it seemed to add to Cotton Mather's reputation as a holy man. But not everyone in Boston believed in witches and at least one man thought poor Margaret was a fraud. Fortunately this man, whose name was Robert Calef (he called himself a merchant, but Mather called him a "weaver"), had the courage to speak his mind, even to write down his opinions. He had observed Margaret, had watched the Mathers try to "save" her, and he thought the whole affair was an outrage. He sat down at once and wrote a detailed and somewhat lurid letter to Cotton Mather, giving his own version of what he had seen in Margaret's home. But Mather refused to reply to him. Mather had written a book called *Wonders of the Invisible World,* to which Calef wrote an answer entitled *More Wonders of the Invisible World.* Calef, in his book, although he vowed that he too believed that witches did exist, carefully contradicted the whole Mather theory of witches and their familiar spirits.

Like nearly everyone who tries to tell the truth when the majority of the people are endorsing a lie, Calef received an angry response. Cotton Mather had him arrested for slander but Calef hastened to express respect for Mather's character and his holy work, and so Mather did not press the charge. Boston printers had refused to publish Calef's book. And when, with the help of a leading Boston merchant named William Brattle, Calef did have his work put into print, Increase Mather burned it in the yard of Harvard College. Still, little by little the book was circulated and more and more thoughtful people were persuaded by it. Here and there other men and women began to raise their heads and question, if not the theory of witchcraft, at least the conduct of the trials at Salem. Cotton Mather himself continued to criticize those trials for their use of "spectral" evidence and for their allowing the names of accused people to be made public.

Judge Samuel Sewall repented openly of his part in the Salem trials

Judge Samuel Sewall, one of the magistrates who had come from Boston to judge the accused witches, repented openly of his part in the trial. On Fast Day 1697, he handed to the pastor of the Old South Church a petition he had written accepting the "blame and the shame" for what he had done in Salem and asking pardon for his error from both man and God. While the pastor read the petition, the judge stood in his pew with his head bowed and with all eyes turned toward him. Only one other, of all those who played an active part in the affair, had courage enough to do public penance. Ann Putnam, who, at the age of twelve had been one of the "afflicted children" who had made the original accusation, stood up in the church at Salem Village fourteen years later and made a public confession that she had acted "ignorantly" and had been "deluded by Satan" into accusing innocent women.

The minister of the Salem Church, one Nicholas Noyes, who had been a leading witch-hunter and who had refused even to comfort the children of one condemned witch who had had their dinner taken away from them by the sheriff, suffered a change of heart eventually and devoted himself it was said to "good works."

It may seem strange that the province that gave birth to the spirit of freedom and the very city (Boston) that was to become known as the "hotbed of liberty" should play a leading part in the suppression of freedom and the violation of individual rights. (Boston had to share the blame because four of the five Salem judges came from Boston.) But the witchcraft tragedy persisted in Massachusetts history as a warning of what might happen if the rights even of an "obviously guilty" person were not protected. It helped educate the citizens of the colony to the need for laws that would guarantee to everyone the right to have a lawyer, to be protected from forced confessions, and to question his accusers. It taught the judges to avoid taking part in a prosecution and to hear both sides of every argument and to try not to be swayed by popular hysteria. Thus, while the price that was paid was a dear and a bitter one, the lessons that were learned were valuable too.

And even in the fever of the trials themselves, while families were looking fearfully at their neighbors, while self-appointed witch-hunters were pouncing on even the tiniest scraps of evidence, and while the great majority of the citizens were clamoring for more blood, there stood out several fearless souls who seemed to embody the true spirit that would one day stand up and fight for freedom. A young Salem man named Joseph Putnam, himself a member of the family that took the lead in exposing the "witches," dared to take a stand against the whole witch business right from the start. He said he did not accept the "evidence" or the testimony of the hysterical children and he refused to believe that his own gentle neighbors were in league with the Devil. Talk like this was dangerous. For less than this other people in the village had already been condemned. But Joseph Putnam, although afraid, would not back down. He always kept loaded guns at his side, to protect himself from seizure. He kept horses in his stable, saddled and ready to ride, in case he had to run for it. And he kept right on saying out loud that the proceedings were based on falsehoods. And fortunately there was no one in town who dared to try to seize him.

In Boston at least one man of God, Joshua Moody, preaching the sermon on Election Day 1692, urged those who had been accused of witchcraft to run away from Salem and hide from their persecutors. He apparently knew well enough that they could not expect a fair trial. And William Brattle, who later helped Robert Calef publish his book, wrote a letter during the witchcraft trials in which he expressed his belief that the evidence was false and that the whole notion of witchcraft was nonsense. This letter, however, was seen by only a few until many years later.

In Andover, Massachusetts, there was a witchcraft panic equal to that in Salem, with a great many innocents in jail where they had to live like animals, with no heat, with only straw to bed down in, and with little food. But here the two ministers of the town stood up together and denounced the persecutions. The two ministers, Francis Dane and Thomas Bernard, joined with thirty citizens who had suffered from the witch-hunt, and together they all petitioned the General Court for payment of damages. Francis Dane spoke out with particular vigor against the manner in which women and even children were forced to confess to "sins" they had never committed. Had he been anything less than a respected leader of the church, he might himself have been seized and jailed, even beaten by the people who had been roused to wild anger against all witches and their defenders. But he said what he had to say and before many years had passed, his fellow townsmen were proud that he had had the courage to restrain them from putting all those innocents to death.

Undoubtedly there were many other men and women of smaller fame who were revolted by the cruelties and falsehoods of the witch trials. But in such times it takes unusual courage to try to oppose an aroused people who have been stirred by fanatical leaders and who have already tasted blood.

4 Wars with the French

The Province of Massachusetts, while it was founded by men and women from England and used the English language and English laws, did have from the earliest days a sprinkling of people from other lands. In 1685, a number of people arrived from France, seeking freedom from religious oppression. These were Huguenots, Protestant Christians who had fled their homeland, where the Catholic Church was the official church and where they were not allowed to worship as they wanted to. The Puritan English in Massachusetts, sympathizing with their plight, welcomed them and allowed them to settle in the province. They were even permitted to enjoy all the rights of Englishmen, provided only that they took an oath of allegiance. Ministers in Boston helped raise money to feed and clothe them, for many of the newcomers had left everything behind.

At first these new arrivals were to be settled along the outer edges of the Province, where they could open up new land and help provide a barrier against the Indians. But these French were largely city people and after a vain attempt to start a new life in the inland area, they nearly all came back to live in and around Boston. Their names then became linked with those of the founders of the colony and some of their names still live in the history of Massachusetts—names such as Bowdoin, Faneuil, Chardon, Sigourney, and Paul Revere. Some of the names became changed into English form very quickly. Paul Revere's father, for instance, had called himself La Rivoire. And some of them have become old Yankee names, marking families that have

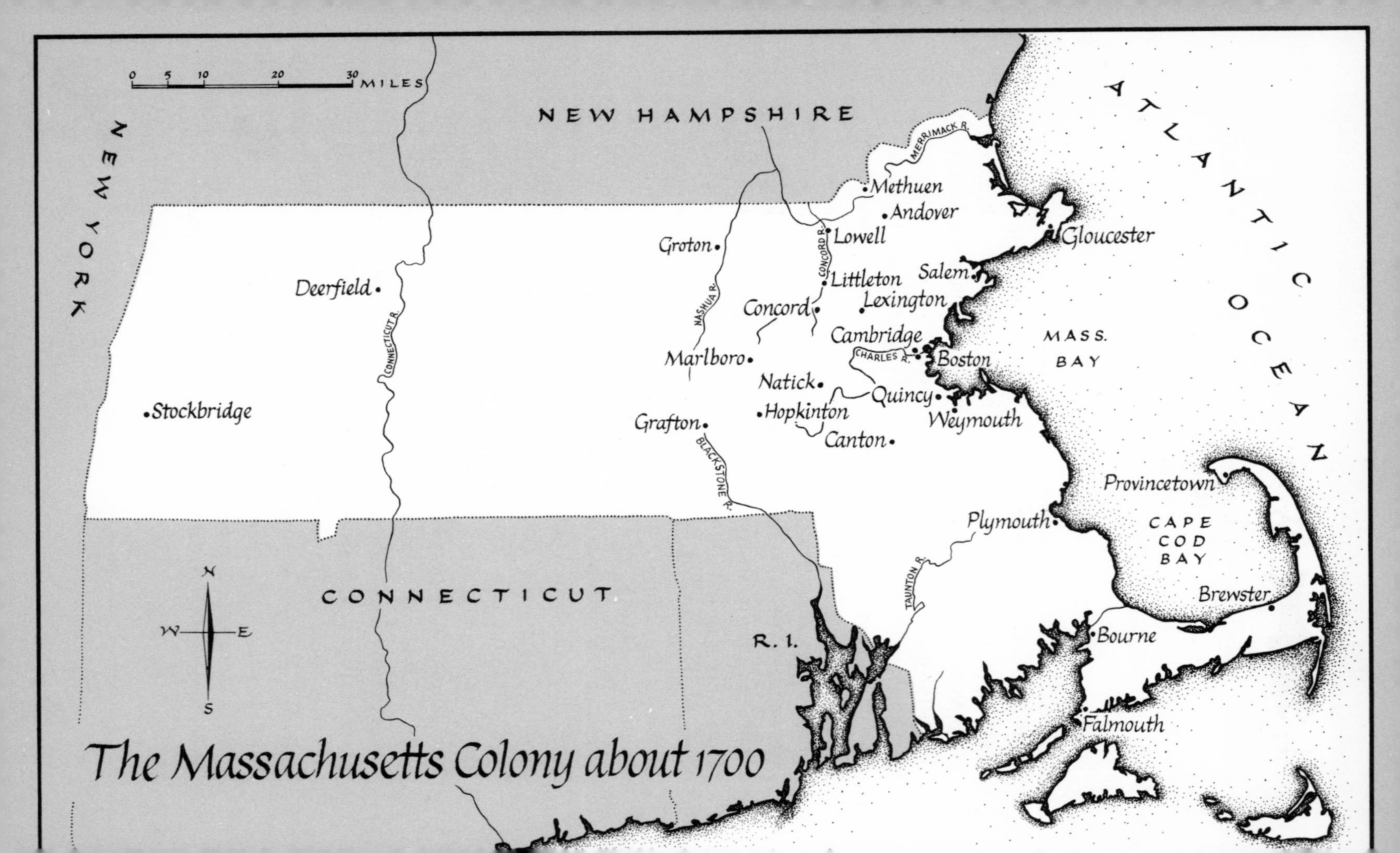

The Massachusetts Colony about 1700

lived in New England since soon after it was founded. Such typical New England names as Larrabee and Fessenden and Lisherness were all of French origin—Lisherness probably having started out in life as La Jeunesse.

The relations with the Canadian French, however, were never so friendly, chiefly because Massachusetts men wanted to have the fur trading posts and fishing grounds all to themselves. There was always disagreement over the boundary of Maine. And for a time, when there were two rival governors in Acadia—one Catholic and one Huguenot—one French governor was always trying to enlist the help of the English settlers against the other. There was constant quarreling, with the Abnaki Indians, many of whom had been converted by Catholic missionaries, fighting on the side of the French.

The long conflict between France and England was not always carried to American soil. Often the Massachusetts people felt that the war was not their affair and at one time the rival kings themselves had agreed that the French and British colonies in America should remain neutral. But there were plenty of things to fight about in America. For one thing, there was the fear and hatred of the "Popish" church, a fear that was almost part of the Puritan religion. There were threats to restore a Catholic monarch to the throne of England which might mean the end of the Congregational Church; and there was the feeling among Catholics in Canada that the Protestant New Englanders were preachers of heresy and little better than non-believers. But the most bitter conflict was always over the right to fish in the wonderful fishing grounds off the coast of Newfoundland, Cape Breton Island, and Maine, and the right to trade with the Indians along the rivers and coasts of Maine and New Hampshire.

Once some Boston men enlisted the aid of the Dutch, who happened at the time to be at war with France while

England was at peace. In a vessel with a Dutch flag they sailed up and down the coasts of Maine and Massachusetts, capturing trading posts, and seizing French ships—all on the pretext of protecting Dutch interests there. But most of the time the tough men who sailed the seas or walked the woods in Maine needed no excuse to try to push out the French so they could extend their own government farther and farther to the east—that is, toward what we now call New Brunswick and Nova Scotia.

The English settlers had never had any plan to live with the Indians or to share the same lands. When they bought or seized land from the Indians, they did not allow the Indians to continue to hunt and camp on it—and this sometimes surprised the Indians, who did not always understand what was meant by "buying" a piece of land. So the Abnaki were gradually pushed off their cornfields and made to depend entirely on the fur trade for their lives. The English had the best goods to trade with them. But the French treated the Indians better. The French lived among the Indians, built forts where the Indians could find safety, made binding agreements with them, learned their language, and offered them the comfort of the Frenchman's religion.

As a result, the Indians generally were more inclined to side with the French when fighting began. Having fewer and fewer fields of their own to grow things on, they were quick to raid the English farm lands, especially when they had French guns and French soldiers to help them. War was to them one way of making a living or increasing their wealth. They always counted on robbing their prisoners of all their goods, even the clothes off their backs.

In the early fighting with the French and their Indian allies, the Massachusetts people had been chiefly concerned with keeping their homes safe from sudden raids, and their fishing boats secure from attack on the water. But when fighting resumed, in 1744, the entire colony seemed in danger. By this time the French had built forts that threatened the inland section of Massachusetts, that part that reached almost to the valley of the Hudson River. There were some who believed the French would eventually own all of America, because they had been so successful in building their forts along the edges of the British colonies and in winning the alliance of the Indians. In 1750, if a man tried to go from Pennsylvania into the country we now call Ohio, he would have found leaden plates fastened to the trees, warning him that he was entering French territory. For French explorers had laid claim to all the land from the Great Lakes to New Orleans. This was bound to cause trouble because when the first British charters were given out they gave to the early colonists the title to all the land beginning at the Atlantic Ocean and extending straight across to the Pacific.

But Massachusetts never really had a chance to press its claim for land as far away as that. The Province of New York, taken from the Dutch, reached up the Hudson, behind Massachusetts and eventually Massachusetts and New York had an argument over where the dividing line should be.

In 1744, however, Massachusetts and New York were about to make common cause again the French, whose forts on the lakes now called Lake George and Lake Champlain and the fort at Niagara were a threat to both colonies. The Massachusetts people felt they never could be safe until all Canada had been taken from the French and this was their constant aim in the warfare that opened at this time. The first move that Massachusetts made was to try to capture the great French fort at Louisbourg, on Cape Breton Island, from which ships could sail out to drive the New Englanders away from the fishing banks, or where warships could gather and be supplied for an attack on Boston.

The colonists of Massachusetts did not look for help from England to stage this attack. They had long ago learned to rely on their own guns and ships and soldiers to fight off any enemy. They were glad when the mother country could help them. But they did not wait around until help arrived. The Englishmen in Massachusetts were different from the common Englishmen at home in that almost every one of them owned a gun and knew how to use it. One of the big holidays in Boston every year was "Training Day," in which all the young men gathered in uniforms with guns or swords or pikes and went through drills in the use of weapons. Right from the start, each colonist had learned to do his own hunting and fighting, and because guns were always so handy the men in Massachusetts were probably somewhat too quick to resort to shooting to settle disputes. And so when King George went to war with France, the Bay soldiers, as the Massachusetts troops were called, did not need to be urged to strike a blow against the enemy.

While many people ridiculed the notion of Governor William Shirley of Massachusetts that colonial ships and troops could capture the stronghold at Louisbourg, the Massachusetts General Court quickly gave its consent and agreed to pay the soldiers and lay out the money for shipping and supplies. A French expedition from Louisbourg had already captured one of the English forts in Nova Scotia, so the colonists felt their danger was great. The neighboring colonies of New Hampshire, Rhode Island and Connecticut were asked to help and each of them voted to send soldiers. Connecticut sent 500 and the other two sent 300 each. Massachusetts sent 3,250 soldiers.

The leader of the expedition was Sir William Pepperrell of Kittery, Maine. Commodore Warren, commander of the British fleet in American waters, agreed to help by sending thirteen armed vessels. They started the siege of

After more than a month of continuous fighting, the French commander surrendered Louisbourg

Louisbourg on May 7, 1745. On June 14, after continuous fighting, the French commander surrendered. (It later turned out that a great stroke of luck helped the colonists win this victory. A warship carrying reinforcements and supplies had been about to leave France in time to save the fort when it caught fire and burned right down to the water, so Louisbourg never received any help.) There was great rejoicing in New England and Old England after the fall of Louisbourg. The people of Massachusetts now assumed that all of Acadia, including Cape Breton Island, would belong to England and their fishing grounds would be protected forever. The soldiers who fought the battle were less than happy however. While only one hundred and thirty of them lost their lives, compared to a loss of three hundred Frenchmen, those who survived felt that they had been treated unfairly. In those days it was always considered a soldier's right to plunder the cities he helped conquer. Many a soldier who signed up for the expedition did so in hope that he might bring home a bag full of booty. But the commander would permit no plundering and the soldiers sailed home empty handed. And the whole colony was dismayed a few years later when, at the peace of Aix-la-Chapelle, England gave Louisbourg back to France in exchange for a city named Madras, in far-off India. This struck Massachusetts as a very poor bargain indeed, and many a man swore to himself never to take up arms for the king again.

The victory had cost Massachusetts more than a quarter million dollars. (The dollar, a Spanish gold coin, was already the favorite piece of money in the American colonies. A British pound was worth from four to six of these coins.)

To placate the Massachusetts colonists the British government voted to reimburse the colony for the money it had spent and soon sent to Boston two hundred chests full of Spanish dollars and one hundred casks full of copper coins. This windfall helped the colony to fulfill all its promises to the soldiers, to exchange its own paper money for coin, and to get rid of many of the different kinds of paper money that were used in the colony. This made the businessmen happy and it pleased most of those who had money owed to them. But a few men who had put their faith in certain kinds of paper money suddenly found that they were poor. The general effect, however, was a good one and it was easier for the colony to enlist soldiers when the next call came.

The peace was a very short one. In fact the American colonists hardly knew any peace at all, for the French were soon busy encouraging the Indians to raid some of the larger towns in Massachusetts and to rob and put to death as many citizens as they could catch. Sometimes the prisoners might be taken to Canada and held for ransom. This new warfare was not like the old border raids the Massachusetts settlers had known. There were organized attacks on large towns, like Deerfield, Massachusetts, and Schenectady, New York, with wholesale killings and robbery. All the colonies suffered from these raids and they began to plan to join together to defend themselves.

The British government decided that the French forts must be taken if the threats to the frontiers were to cease. Regular troops came from overseas to do battle with the French and their Indian allies. The British had Indian allies, too, chiefly in New York, where the Senecas, the Onandagas, the Tuscaroras, the Oneidas, and the Cayugas had usually favored the British. But the French had also influenced these Indians by their friendliness and their willingness to build strong points where the Indians could find safety, or where they could leave their families under French protection while the men were at war.

The fighting went badly for the British for a long time. They established a fort called William Henry, on the New York frontier. This was attacked and taken by the French and Indians. The French, urging the English forces to surrender, promised them that they would be well treated and would be protected from the Indians. But the Indians, who had their minds on plunder, were not to be restrained. They fell upon the English captives, killed some, and tore the clothes off many of them. Some men fled stark naked into the woods and wandered for days, looking for help. Colonel Frye, commanding the Bay troops, was counted lost, but he turned up many days later, scratched, bitten, and dazed, wearing only his shirt. After this disaster, the colonists were convinced the French would sweep right through the province. All residents west of the Connecticut River were ordered to bring their cattle in from pasture and destroy all their wheel wagons, lest the enemy make use of them.

The French did not come, however, and winter put an end to the fighting for that year. The following spring the British decided to take Fort Ticonderoga, on Lake Champlain, which they heard was weakly defended. Bay troops and regulars, sixteen thousand strong, moved up through the forest and over Lake George, led by General James Abercrombie. Many soldiers took ill along the way in the rain and chill of late April. One soldier's journal tells of a comrade who was seized with a "fever nago" (which was his way of spelling "fever and ague"). But despite difficulties the British force made its way in good time toward the unsuspecting Frenchmen at Ticonderoga. They crossed Lake George in a great flotilla, on a clear starry night, when the surface of the water was like dark velvet, without a wind stirring. In the lead was a large boat carrying young Lord William Howe, the second in command. Behind him came the great convoy, the British regulars in the center, with the boats carrying the Bay troops on either side. They had wound the oarlocks with cloth to keep them from squeaking and they moved in almost complete silence through the dark, with only the sound of the dipping oars breaking the stillness. French and Indian scouts on the nearby hills saw not a sign of them as they swept majestically along. But at sunrise, the sudden blaze of the scarlet uniforms alarmed the watchers, who went hurrying off to the fort, about four miles away, to warn of the approach.

If the British had known the woods better, or had they taken the trouble to find the right guides, they might have scored a famous victory. But without any knowledge of how to stay on the track, the troops blundered along through the forest. Lord Howe had sent Major Israel Putnam of Connecticut, with one hundred men, to search out the way and look for the enemy. The French had a small outpost nearby that the French themselves set fire to before retreating. Putnam and his small company chased after them and soon caught them, for the French too had lost their way in the forest. Lord Howe, leading his troops in battle as commanders did in the old days, came along in time to join the fight. But the soldiers on both sides were completely bewildered and had a hard time, in the thick brush, distinguishing friend from foe. They were used to fighting in formation and became quickly confused if their comrades were scattered. The French were badly defeated in the fight, with three hundred killed and one hundred and forty made prisoners. But in the confusion, Lord Howe was shot in the back, most likely by one of his own men, for he was facing the enemy when he died. And the English troops were so scattered, so weary, and so bewildered that they were ordered to return to their landing spot at the head of Lake George, where they camped for the night. They had come within two miles of Ticonderoga when the fight began.

The next day, the British troops returned to the site of the battle and drove off a French force that had come down from the fort. In the morning General Abercrombie had the artillery brought up to the rapids in the stream, where the first skirmish had taken place. But an engineer sent ahead to scout the enemy fortifications brought back the report that the outerworks of the fort were so weak—just a few felled trees—that the British could take them with musket and bayonet. To drag the heavy artillery up through the dense forest would be a task of great difficulty, requiring men to go ahead and slash out a road with their axes. So Abercrombie was easily persuaded to leave his cannon behind and to try to take the fort with cold steel and musket fire. This was a dreadful mistake. When the troops reached the fort, they found it was protected by an embankment eight feet high, made of rocks and earth, with heavy trees felled in front of it so that their tangled tops faced outward toward the attackers. The British and colonial troops charged gallantly into this barricade and began to hack a pathway through the trees. The big brass cannon in the fort blasted right into their faces, killing the attackers by the hundreds. Hardly a man was able to climb the parapet. When five hundred men had been killed, the general ordered his drummers to beat the retreat and the army, after a fight that had lasted ten hours, dragged itself back to the landing place on Lake George, carrying the wounded.

It had been the plan originally to have this force, after taking Ticonderoga, move up Lake Champlain and on into Canada, to join with another British force coming up the St. Lawrence from the sea. But now this plan had to be abandoned. The British could do nothing but hasten back to the other end of Lake George. Two hundred barrels of flour that they had brought along to feed the troops after Ticonderoga had been taken were broken open and dumped on the ground.

Even at Fort William Henry, now repaired and back in British hands, there was no safety. Men who wandered off toward the villages were waylaid and scalped by Indians hiding in the forest. Major Putnam, in the heat of the fighting before Ticonderoga, was captured by an Indian and tied to a tree in the forest, where shots from both sides tore his clothes to ribbons. Yet the major himself received not a scratch. When the English retreated, the Indians, rejoicing to have such a prize in their hands, carried Putnam, with his hands bound tightly together, deep into the forest. They tied him to another tree here and piled dry brush all around him, after having stripped him naked. Then the feathered warriors set fire to the brush and danced around the poor major, singing their death chants. But Putnam must have felt that the Lord was surely watching over him that day. Just as the flames began to mount, there came a sudden drenching shower that nearly put out the fire. And at this point a French officer happened on the scene, rushed through the smoldering brush, untied the terrified major, and took him to safety. Putnam was removed to Canada then, where he was treated with kindness and courtesy and eventually sent home in exchange for a French prisoner. Back in Massachusetts, he organized a group of men to wage guerrilla warfare against French and Indians during the winter.

The British had not always treated the French with kindness. In 1755, worried that the Acadians, who had taken an oath not to oppose the British king, might be persuaded to go back on that promise, the British decided to remove the entire population of "French neutrals" as they were called, and scatter them in places where they could not damage the British cause. Whole villages were rounded up and forced on board transports to be carried west and south. It was a hardhearted move and it caused much indignation and protest. The British were accused of tearing families and sweethearts apart, so that they never found each other again.

Acadians were rounded up and forced into exile

Henry Wadsworth Longfellow, the New England poet, writing of the event a century later, told his story of Evangeline, an Acadian girl who was separated from the man she loved and looked in vain for him all her life. (*Evangeline* is the poem that begins with the famous lines, "This is the forest primeval/ The murmuring pines and the hemlocks / Stand like the Druids of eld . . .") But actually the British were not quite so cruel as legend has made them sound. They made every effort to keep families together and set them in places where they could earn their living. Some, it is true, found it difficult to adjust their ways to the new life and had to be supported by public charity. But many prospered and retained their language and customs through generations. A large number of these Acadians settled in Masschusetts and many more traveled as far as Louisiana, where the 'Cadians or Cajuns are still recognizable as a separate breed.

The British forces suffered defeat after defeat. It seemed as if the French were bound to conquer, to turn all the carefully cultivated farm lands back to the Indians and to move the Popish church into Massachusetts, and make the Puritan church illegal. But the British, as they had so often in their history, came up with an able general, Sir Jeffery Amherst (who gave his name to a college and a town in Massachusetts), who showed them how to turn defeat into victory.

Amherst first led his forces against Louisbourg, which the French had greatly strengthened after it had been given back to them. The British forces landed, under the protection of heavy fire from their warships, and camped before the stronghold. After seven weeks of siege, the fort surrendered for the second time and remained in British hands from that time forth. Meanwhile, after the defeat of Ticonderoga, General Abercrombie was ready to abandon the fight, but Colonel Bradstreet, now second in command, persuaded Abercrombie to let him attack Fort Frontenac on Lake Ontario. By forced marches that tired his troops and caused many to fall sick and a few to die, Bradstreet reached Frontenac before the French soldiers there had any suspicion that he was coming. With hardly a shot fired, Bradstreet made prisoners of all the French he found there, destroyed nine small French ships on the lake, and captured a great deal of food and supplies. Then, hearing that a larger French force was on its way to the fort, Bradstreet led his tired troops back to Albany. In this way they cut the route that the French used to supply the forts farther south, and they deprived those forts of much needed ammunition. These two victories, at Louisbourg and Fort Frontenac, encouraged the English and colonial forces to hope for greater victories the next season.

In the winters of 1757 and 1758, when the Indians under French direction were making sudden attacks in force against the settlements in inland Massachusetts, the colonists had been close to despair. Luckily for them, smallpox had so weakened the Abnaki Indians that there was little danger in the east. But the residents west of the Connecticut River lived in fear. They did, that is, until they learned of Rogers' Rangers—a force of trained woodsmen led by Major Robert Rogers, a New Hampshire man then living in Methuen, Massachusetts. These men, dressed like Indians, in gray jackets, and each carrying a small hatchet or tomahawk and a scalping knife, along with a musket, a powder horn, a compass, and wearing a sealskin belt, slipped through the snowy forests as silently as wolves and often fell without warning on encampments of French and Indians. They succeeded in throwing constant fear into the enemy, too, so that the danger of the raids was greatly diminished.

Then, General Amherst, who had been placed in command of all the forces in America, sailed down from Louisbourg to Boston and camped on the Boston Common. There was always resistance in Boston to the placing of troops (it was called "quartering" them) in the city. There were barracks on Castle Island in the harbor where troops could live. And war or no war, the lawmakers in Massachusetts strongly disapproved of stationing armed soldiers in their capital city. It looked too much as if the home government was trying to frighten the lawmakers themselves into passing only laws the king would approve of.

In 1757, the General Court had refused to allow troops to be quartered in Boston and this had so angered Lord Loudon, who was commanding the troops in New York, that he threatened to march several regiments to the rebellious city. He apparently was not too sure of his ground, however, and he changed his mind about sending the troops. Parliament in England had passed a law permitting the quartering of troops in cities, but the General Court insisted the law did not apply in Massachusetts. Whether it did or not was not decided at this time, but the same disagreement arose some years later and ended in bloodshed.

But when General Amherst brought his triumphant troops into the city, they were greeted joyously. In a short time they marched off, ten thousand strong, to Albany, where they spent the fall and winter getting ready to drive the French off Lake Champlain. The war was won miles away however. General James Wolfe, on June 1, 1759, sailed out of Louisbourg and up the St. Lawrence, with a force of five thousand men, only four hundred of whom were from Massachusetts. The enemy of course knew of his coming and made ready to stop him along the river. Louis Montcalm, the brilliant French commander, always seemed to read the British minds and meet them with great force wherever they tried to move. This time he awaited Wolfe at the Falls of Montmorency on the St. Lawrence River.

Wolfe landed there and attempted to storm the French position, but he could not budge Montcalm. It seemed then that the British would have to acknowledge defeat and sail back down the river without even seeing Quebec, which had been the object of their attack. The summer was dying and freezing weather was almost at hand. Too long a delay would imprison the British ships in these northern waters and mean total disaster. Montcalm must have rejoiced at his foresight in lying in wait for the British here. He had picked out what he felt sure were the three points at which the British would try to land. As for Quebec itself, that, Montcalm had decided, needed only a small force to defend it, for it was safe behind its steep cliffs, two hundred feet high. Unless the enemy has wings, said Montcalm, Quebec is safe.

But this time Montcalm had tried once too often to read the enemy's mind. In war, great generals say, that is a mistake. Instead, one should always figure out what the enemy is *capable* of doing. If you try always to read his intentions, you are sure to be wrong one day.

Montcalm was wrong this time because Wolfe was a determined man who liked to use his brains. He studied the land around Quebec and discovered that there was a narrow path that led up the steep cliffs to the Plains of Abraham, at Quebec. If one man can get up there, he told himself, then five thousand can. So while he kept the enemy busy with a pretense of further attacks at the Falls of Montmorency, he sent twenty-four volunteers to climb the cliffs. They reached the Plains undetected and reported that there was only a small force of Frenchmen there. In the dark and in the gray dawn the painful task began of bringing the men up one by one, then hauling the heavy cannon up on ropes. At eight o'clock on the morning of September 13, the entire army was on the Plains, with all its artillery, and they quickly killed or captured the few

Montcalm's troops could not withstand the onslaught of Wolfe's forces, and when the battle ended, Quebec was in British hands

French soldiers that had been left there as guards. Montcalm received the news too late. With five thousand men he hastened to stand between Wolfe's men and the city, but the English were now in a strong position and could not be stopped. In the fierce battle that followed Montcalm was killed. Wolfe, the hero of the day, was wounded three times and would not live, but the British owned the mighty fort of Quebec and commanded the gateway to Canada.

With Wolfe dead and a less skilful general in command, the French tried to win back the city with three thousand Canadian troops and four hundred Indians. They nearly caught the new British commander, General James Murray, asleep, and they arrived on the Plains of Abraham only a short time after the alarm had been given. More than a thousand British soldiers were lost in the battle that followed and only the timely arrival of British warships in the river below the fort forced the French to pull out and move farther up the river, to Montreal.

To save Quebec, Montcalm had pulled most of his troops away from the forts on Lake Champlain, and when Amherst approached with his ten thousand fresh soldiers, the French abandoned the forts at Crown Point and Ticonderoga and blew them up before the British arrived. Meanwhile, other British troops had taken the forts on Lake Ontario and then all the forces met to proceed along the St. Lawrence toward Montreal. It was a difficult and costly journey with many boats wrecked in the swift water and more than eighty soldiers drowned. But when the British forces drew up outside Montreal, the French commander saw his situation was hopeless and after a short parley, he surrendered. That practically ended the war, left England in control of Canada, and finally made the borders of Massachusetts secure.

There was more fighting between England and France the following year and some Massachusetts troops even took part in a successful attack on Havana, Cuba (because Spain, which owned Cuba, had taken the side of France). But the fighting against the French had ended for the men of New England. The Indians were largely pacified and the Massachusetts men, about one out of five of whom had served in the war, were able to till their farm lands or cast their fishnets in peace.

The French and Indian War taught the Massachusetts people many lessons. They learned that, while they might not have been so well disciplined as the British regulars, they were the equals of the regulars on the battlefield and superior to the regulars in the wilderness. They were more skilled at shooting, too, for they had learned to sight down the barrel of a gun when they fired it, while the British soldier had been taught merely to keep the muzzle of the gun a little lower than the butt. The men from Massachusetts Bay learned also that it was possible to fight the Indian by his own methods, by sneaking through the woods in small groups, to fall without warning on an encampment. Robert Rogers and Israel Putnam both led groups of forest fighters that used Indian tactics in this war with great success.

The people of Massachusetts also realized that they would have to spend their own blood and their own treasure to keep their land safe. And they discovered ways of working together with the other American colonies, through Assemblies to which all the colonies were invited to send delegates. And the soldiers who traveled miles from home to fight side by side with men of other faiths and other backgrounds probably learned to be less prejudiced against those who went to different churches, traced their parentage to another land, or ate dishes that Massachusetts men had no stomach for.

Unsettled, but still stirring in colonial minds, was the question of whether or not the Parliament in London could pass laws that bound the colonists to obedience. The fact that they had to capture Louisbourg twice caused many a colonist to wonder if the English king was really much concerned with the welfare of the colonies, when his own was not endangered. And there was still the question of the great expanse of land in the broad valley of the Mississippi River, many thousands of square miles, to which the French still held title. To the Indian this was bewildering.

"The French claim the land west of the mountains," one Indian said. "And the English claim all the land on the east. Where is the Indian's land?"

5 White Hands & Black Hands

The wealth of Massachusetts lay at first in its fish, its furs, its timber, its metals, and its soil. The home government very early drew up a list of harmful trades which it did not want established in the colony. These included all manufactures that would compete with the trades of the mother country—chiefly the spinning of thread, the weaving of cloth, and the making of things out of hides. All finished goods—clothing, shoes, canvas for sails, nails, bullets, blankets, linens, dishes, kettles, spoons, knives, yard goods, glasses, lamps, and guns were in the early years carried back from overseas in ships that brought spars, staves, whale oil, raw wool, beef, and fish to England. Even the ships, according to the early Navigation Acts, had to be English ships with English crews. And trade was not permitted with France, Spain, and Holland, or their colonies, except on payment of heavy duties.

So from the very beginning, the men and women of Massachusetts lived largely by the fruit of their own hands—the corn they grew in their own gardens, the cattle they raised, the game they shot in the forests, the timber they chopped down, and the fish they drew out of the sea. Soon, however, dependence on the mother country became impossible; and the temptation to trade off their natural wealth for the treasures of other nations nearby became too strong. Boston then became a center for trade, or the ex-

The itinerant traders of early colonial times were gradually replaced by merchants with established shops

change of one kind of goods for another; and its wealthy men were the merchants who accepted the local products and exchanged them for goods from other lands—then sold those goods in their shops. These men, from being mere buyers and sellers, gradually extended their interests to the actual manufacture of material they needed in their work, and the ownership of the vessels that carried their products across the sea.

Merchants then became owners of shipyards and rope-walks, where men walked up and down in sheds as long as three city blocks, to twist hempen threads into ropes and cables many fathoms long. (A fathom is a measure used by sailors in reckoning the depth of water. Originally it was the measure from finger-tips to finger-tips of a grown man's arms when fully extended on each side. Then it became standardized at six feet.) Merchants not only owned the wharfs where ships unloaded but they rented out the shops built on the wharfs, owned fishing vessels and even ships that hunted the sperm whale in all the seas of the world. And what they depended on most, besides the natural riches in land and sea, was the labor of men and women who spun the hemp; hammered out the metal fittings that went on masts and sails and spars, cast the nets and lines into the sea; worked the ships and harpooned the mighty whales; cut the trees to make masts, spars, and even firewood for the forges; dug the metal out of the earth, melted it in the roaring furnaces; tanned the hides; herded the cattle; tilled the soil; gathered the shellfish; and performed all the small daily tasks that enabled a busy town to get up in the morning, do its business in proper season, and find its way safely to bed at night.

Out in the small villages in the inland sections, families lived mostly on farms, unless they preached the Gospel, taught school, or dealt out justice in the courts. In Boston and the few large towns by the sea, lived most of the hand laborers and artisans—the leather-apron crowd who swung hammers and axes, put ships and houses together, and prepared the drink and food. These were the caulkers (who drove strips of tarred rope in between the planking of a ship to make it watertight), the joiners (carpenters who knew how to fit boards and planks tightly together and nail them securely), the chandlers (who dipped string into wax to make candles so men could see after dark), the cordwainers (shoemakers), the drovers (who goaded the oxen through the streets), the smiths (who swung the hammers that shaped metal into nails, horseshoes, and even silverplate), the butchers, the brewers, and the sailors, as well as the more gentle handworkers who baked bread, shaved whiskers, fashioned wigs, and made or mended clothing.

It was these thousands of busy hands that really built the fortunes that began to grow in Massachusetts, until there was not a luxury in the old country that could not be matched in the new. Many of the hands were thick with calluses, or reddened raw by wind and sea. Many were blackened by soot or charcoal or grease. And many were black because they belonged to black men who had been captured in Africa and brought here to be sold as slaves. Soon after the colony had ships and trade of its own, there were black Americans there as well as white Americans, contributing their own sweat and toil to the growth of the nation, even taking up arms to help beat off its enemies.

Many of the black people had no family names at all, for their owners just gave them short names they could know them by—Cato and Adam and Doll and Ned. The records of early Massachusetts are full of such names, many of them still used after the person had been freed. Listed as an able-bodied sailor in a ship, the *Prince of Orange,* that helped guard the coast of America in the early 1700's is a black man named Syphax, who had no other name.

Many slaves in the colony were set free by their masters, who could perhaps not get used to the idea of having another man do all the unpleasant work. Hard work, according to the Puritan religion, was the lot of all true Christians, white or black, and it was nothing to be ashamed of or to be avoided. Still the disgraceful buying and selling of slaves continued in Boston right to the time the province won its freedom. The local papers carried advertisements of new "lots" of black people, brought in filthy crowded ships from Africa, to be sold like horses or cattle in a public square or in a store. There were men whose job it was to sort out the slaves, taking the sickly and the weak to one side, and putting only the healthy and strong up for sale. Sometimes the others were given away to any who would take them.

Yet the black men, slave as well as free, who worked in Boston were among the earliest and angriest fighters for freedom from the oppression of the British Crown. Leader of a riotous demonstration against the soldiers in 1770 was an escaped slave—part Indian, part English, part African—by the name of Crispus Attucks and he was the first American to fall before British gunfire.

There were white men in Massachusetts in the 1700's who had no special skill, who were not carpenters, nor shipbuilders, nor wheelwrights, nor blacksmiths, nor bakers, nor tailors, nor makers of candles or candle sticks. They worked on the small farms or along the waterfront, tending cattle and sheep, mending wharfs, loading and unloading ships, making rope, firing up forges in the copper works, pushing handbarrows loaded with firewood, or peddling charcoal from carts, or sweeping chimneys, working as waiters in the taverns, spreading pebbles on the streets, killing steers for market, or sailing out in the fishing vessels or the whaling or trading ships. Many of them lived as poor as the black people did, shared their tables with the blacks, and worked alongside them on wharf and ship. These men too were among the first to feel the urge to strike an angry blow in the name of Liberty. And on their side were the rowdy apprentices and servants, the hardworking, poorly fed and shabbily clothed young men and boys who liked to do mischief in the streets, to fight, play football, or steal a few delicacies now and then. None of these people could pose for statues or fine paintings, nor could they make fine speeches. But their hard work helped make the province richer. And their reckless desire for liberty helped put the province in a mood to fight for it.

There was a wide difference, in the town of Boston and in a few of the larger towns—Worcester, Cambridge, Roxbury, Salem, Plymouth, and the like—between the comfortable people and the poor. Wealthy as Boston was, there could be found families there that lived in one room—man, wife and several children, without clothes enough to keep warm, and only a few chips of wood to keep a fire going in the fireplace. But Massachusetts people generally made a point of looking after the poor, even though there were some people in that day who thought that it was only laziness—and not illness or lack of learning or bad luck—that made a man poor. The religion of rich and poor was usually the same, although after the vote was extended to freeholders other religions, even the Quakers and the Baptists, were allowed to settle in Boston and build their churches (or "meeting houses") there.

The one religion that was not given leave to hold public services was the Roman Catholic Church, for the authorities of the province still wanted no "Popish" priests among them. Still, there were a number of Irish Catholics, ragged and hardhanded laborers many of them, who also yearned for a chance to fight against the Crown, especially after King George III began to look for ways to lay taxes on the colonists to fatten his own purse. And when the fighting did begin, the scorned "Irish teagues" (teague was an insulting nickname given to Irishmen) were found mostly carrying muskets or manning ships on the side of freedom. And some who came over with the king's troops ran away to find homes in this new land and never leave it.

6 Games and Pastimes

The Puritans of Massachusetts had very few holidays. They did not celebrate Christmas. In fact they forbade its celebration. Holly wreaths, Christmas trees, feasting, singing carols, the giving of gifts, and the burning the Yule log were pagan doings, the Puritan fathers believed, and they would not permit them in the colony.

The Puritans did hold a Thanksgiving each season at about the time of harvest, when there was feasting and prayer. They acknowledged the king's birthday with the firing of cannon and the drinking of toasts. (But some of them were violently opposed to the flying of the English flag, because it wore the red "Cross of Rome" in its center. One leading citizen actually cut the cross out of the flag when he found it displayed in public.) The major holidays were the days on which elections were held—one to elect the councillors and representatives to the General Court and the other to elect officers in the artillery company. There was also a Training Day, much relished by the young men, when there was marching and riding and shooting at targets and other military drill.

But 'Lection Days, as they were called, usually provided the longest celebrations, and they were the days the children of the colony enjoyed the most. Voting was usually done in a public square or open field. In Boston it was done on the Common. There were speeches and arguments, and sometimes actual fist-fights. Booths were set up where cakes were sold. And of course there were places where the grown-ups could buy their rum. The governor was escorted to

Thanksgiving, a day of feasting and prayer, was one of the few

holidays that the Puritans celebrated

the Town House by a parade. There was always a sermon given in which the sins of the province were counted over and the citizens were called upon to mend their ways.

In Boston there were two special holidays that were much valued by the young people of the town—and by many who were no longer young. These were Commencement—when the graduates of Harvard College received their degrees—and Pope Day, which was the New England version of Guy Fawkes Day. (In Old England, Guy Fawkes Day marks the arrest of Guy Fawkes, a Roman Catholic who once plotted to blow up Parliament with gunpowder. On this day, children burn "guys"—stuffed dummies—in bonfires.) The Pope was much feared in New England. All properly bred boys were raised on readings of the Bible and passages from Foxe's *Book of Martyrs,* which related the sufferings of the Protestant martyrs at the hands of the Catholic Church. Until the Acadians were brought into the colony in 1755, there were hardly any Catholics in Massachusetts, so children were brought up knowing only that the Roman Church had long ago burned Protestants at the stake. The Pope, they were taught, was in league with the Devil.

On Commencement Day, which usually came on a Wednesday, men and women and young people would gather from all over Boston and Cambridge (where the college was located) and even from towns several miles away, to rejoice at the completion of the school year. The students themselves of course did much of the celebrating, with drinking and singing and practical jokes. But friends and relatives joined in too, much as they do today, attending banquets, playing games, parading, and singing. Invariably the celebrations continued for the rest of the week, so that for many people this proved the grandest holiday of the year—four or five days of rejoicing, of merriment, of idleness, feasting, and greeting of friends from far away, with bonfires and bright lights and even fireworks when it grew dark.

But to the rowdy boys of Boston there was nothing to match Pope Day. There were two rival gangs in the town, one from the South End (which would be the area around the Common and including Milk, School, and Summer streets and the waterfront from Dorchester Neck to the South Battery at the foot of Broad Street) and one from the North End (which would be all that area north of the canal or creek that ran right across the town where Blackstone Street now runs). Each gang would make its own "pope" out of paper, with a light inside. And there would also be a paper devil to stand behind the pope and prod him with his pitchfork. Sometimes there would be an effigy on a gallows of the pretender, Charles Edward, grandnephew of Charles II who in 1670 had tried to betray England into the hands of the Catholic Majesty of France. The figure of the pope was fixed on a pole so it could be raised up to peer into upstairs windows in the town. All the figures would be set on the platform of a cart, drawn by horses or oxen, with boys dressed in wild costumes riding alongside or following in a ragged parade. Sometimes the leader of the gang would go first, riding a donkey and wearing a mask or some outrageous costume. All along the path of the parade, firecrackers would be set off, and boys carrying little bells in their hands would go from door to door in the manner of the "trick-or-treaters" of a later day and sing, when their knocks were answered, this traditional song:

Remember, remember, the Fifth of November
The Gunpowder Treason and Plot.
I see no reason why Gunpowder Treason
Should ever be forgot . . .

. . . .

Don't you hear my little bell go chink, chink, chink?
Please to give me a little coin
To buy my pope some drink.

At nearly every door the boys would receive a few coins that would go into the same bag. Then, at the close of the day, the two gangs would meet at Union Street—neutral ground between the North End and the South End. Here they could lay into each other with fist, club, and even stones—a real gang war—until one side had captured the "pope" that belonged to the other. The victor would get *all* the funds that had been collected and would spend it on a wild celebration. If the South End gang won, the "popes" would be taken either to the Common or to the gallows on Dorchester Neck and burned in a tremendous bonfire, while the gang members danced about singing, drinking, and bragging of their victory. If the North End won, the celebration and bonfire would be held on Copps Hill, overlooking the harbor in the direction of Charlestown.

There were of course less reckless games than this that were played by the boys of Massachusetts. But the favorite game, football, was almost as bloody as the Pope Day fight. This was usually played in the late fall in Boston, whenever anyone could get a pig's bladder that could be stuffed with something and kicked along the street. There were no special rules to this game except that the ball had to be propelled by kicking it. Any number of boys could play and sometimes there would be as many as fifty on a side.

Games that provided an excuse for gambling—card playing, horse racing, quoits, bowling, dice, and the like were all frowned upon by the Puritan church, and for a long time public taverns were forbidden to keep cards or quoits or dice or bowling pins anywhere about the premises. But of course people would still enjoy such pastimes on the quiet. And in every part of the province horses were raced from time to time. When British soldiers came to occupy Boston, one of the complaints against them was that they kept young people away from church by racing their horses on the Common.

In the countryside, the colonists would often make games out of work. A husking bee was a favorite autumn entertainment, and it was one way for a farmer to get all his corn husked and made ready for the mill in a single evening. The freshly picked corn would all be heaped on the barn floor while young people were seated around it, boys and girls alternating. At a signal the husking would begin, each person grabbing an ear, stripping the covering from it and breaking the cob free from the last bit of stem. If a young man found a red ear—and Indian corn would often turn red when ripe—he could kiss every girl in the ring. If a girl found a red ear, she could pick out her favorite from the young men and kiss him. And the person who husked the final ear would be declared winner of the contest. This system kept the young people scrambling to grab up one ear after another. Usually there were jugs of freshly made cider, not aged enough to be intoxicating, passed around the circle.

The married ladies of the neighborhood might hold a quilting bee that could be accompanied by singing and cider-drinking too, and by gossip. Each lady would bring heaps of rags and clippings, left over from the making of clothes, to be sewn together into a crazy pattern of many different colors, to make a large square bag that would be stuffed with rags, then "quilted" or fastened together in small squares to keep the rags from bunching up in one end or the other. This would become a bed cover and every household would own a number of them.

Mixed dancing and stage plays were for many years severely frowned on in Massachusetts. Indeed, there was no real theater in Boston until long after the Revolution. Still some plays were occasionally presented. While students at Harvard could be severely punished for taking part in any public theatrical entertainment, they did occasionally manage to stage a play in private, before an audience of teachers

A quilting party in colonial New England

and college officials. And when the British occupied Boston, after the Battles of Lexington and Concord, Gentleman Johnny Burgoyne, the British general, wrote a play that was presented in public in Boston. (Burgoyne delayed his departure from the town in order to attend the performance.)

There were other forms of recreation that the Puritans never objected to, as long as they were not indulged in on the Sabbath. Fishing, besides being a major business in the province, was also a favorite recreation for people of every station. One governor of Massachusetts, notorious for his stinginess, did not think it beneath his dignity to take a rowboat out among the islands in Boston harbor to fish for tom cod, a plentiful small fish, a cousin of the famous fish on which so much income depended. The governor's enemies used to mutter that tom cod was all that was ever served at the governor's table. There was fishing in every part of the province, for Massachusetts is full of small ponds and lakes, and in the early days, with so much of the forest uncut, there were hundreds more small streams and larger rivers where fish were found.

Hunting was a steady occupation of the early dwellers in the colony and it remained a recreation even when the pressing need of game for food was no longer felt. The great green forest that reached from the western shore of the Connecticut River for fifty miles into the Berkshire Hills, was alive with small and large animals and with wildfowl of all kinds that required skill and patience to find and kill. Even the stretches of hardwood trees close by the towns held game enough to make them worth hunting through. Every country boy and many of those from the small towns knew how to load and aim a gun, and many of them, when they grew up, would startle the British regulars with their marksmanship.

Young people who lived along the shores of Maine and Massachusetts made frequent trips to the rocks and islands that lay nearby. Here they would hunt gull's eggs, or find clams and oysters and crabs, or gather up at low tide the tawny rockweed that grew under high water and bring it home to be cooked down into ash called "kelp" that made fine fertilizer. On such trips they often brought baskets with food and drink, so that they could picnic on some distant beach. Swimming, however, was not much thought of. Even sailors who worked ships that traveled nearly around the world might not be able to save themselves if they fell into water over their heads. Proper people might wade out more than knee deep into the water, for sport, but they would not think of plunging half-clothed into the waves.

To many residents, the Great and Thursday Lecture, where one of the ministers would often explain to them the relation of the Scriptures to their daily lives, provided a refreshing break in the routine. And there were other events that would serve in place of stage plays. A great horseman might give exhibitions of his skill—riding two or three steeds in tandem, or leaping on a horse in full gallop, or performing gymnastic and balancing feats on horseback.

Occasionally someone might bring a white bear or some other outlandish animal to town and put it on exhibition for a shilling admission. And once someone in Boston set up a small model of Jerusalem and asked people to pay to observe it. (Those who did, came away feeling that they had been cheated.)

Men with good voices sometimes undertook to present a whole opera individually, speaking some parts and singing others. Or they would read whole plays or other works of literature to as many as a hundred people at a time. Therefore, residents of the towns did not feel they were being deprived altogether of cultural experience, particularly as there was a constant shower of pamphlets from the local printers, pretending sometimes to be "letters" from some distinguished, unnamed gentleman, to a local inhabitant, giving views on taxes, liberty, the Gospel, witchcraft, or the rights of man. Letter writing, especially among certain well-placed ladies, was a special art. Most of the letters were written in an artificial, wordy style, to show off the writer's learning. But such writing was much admired in that day and brought pleasure to writer and recipient, who might read the letters over and over to friends and relatives. There were long hours in the New England winter evenings that could only be spent in quiet pursuits of this kind.

7 Rumblings of Rebellion

Once the war with France had come to an end, King George III of England and his advisers turned their eyes to the American colonies with thoughts of how they might be made to add to the income of the Crown. What appealed to the king the most about an income from America was that it was not likely to cause any unpleasant questions from Parliament over why the money was needed and how it would be spent. There were, after all, no representatives from America, with voters to answer to. And so whatever came into the royal purse from that source might be spent as the king and his closest advisers saw fit.

King George was not really the madman some stories have made him seem. He was a simple man, with a high sense of honor. But he had no experience of and not much patience with democracy. Privately he often yearned to go back to his own small kingdom of Hanover, in Germany, where he was absolute ruler, with no one to question how he spent money or time. When his advisers showed him the advantages of extra income from America, he was immediately in favor of it. He really knew very little about the colonies and never sympathized in the least with their desire to have a voice in taxing themselves. When someone tried once to explain the religion of the people of Massachusetts, he was surprised. "Are they not all Presbyterians?" he asked. And he was shocked to learn that they elected their own ministers. This, he felt sure, would lead to all sorts of evils, so that plain people might even try to unseat a leader they did not agree with.

But when the Crown tried to raise revenue by putting taxes on imports to the colonies, it was as if they had poked a stick into a live nest of hornets. George and his advisers had perhaps not noticed that for many years the people of Massachusetts particularly had insisted on keeping for themselves, or for their General Court, the right to dispose of their own property. And the House of Representatives, the branch of the General Court that was elected by the freeholders, had always considered that the laying of taxes and the paying out of money, such as for the governor's salary, was their "most darling privilege." It was among the basic rights of an Englishman, they argued, to decide for himself how his property was to be used and to pay taxes only when his own representatives had approved them. And just because they were living in America did not make them any less English.

From the start they did not blame the new taxes on the king but on Parliament. Right to the eve of the Revolution they vowed their loyalty to King George. And even when the patriots were gathered, with George Washington in command, outside of Boston, with the English troops besieged inside, some of the patriots called themselves the king's troops and called the British regulars the troops of Parliament. To Englishmen the king was the living body of the British Constitution and the rights of the private subject. The fact that, in actual truth, he was personally supporting all efforts to wring revenue out of America was not immediately clear to the revolutionists.

At the start, the taxes were levied on goods brought into America from sources outside the mother county. Some such taxes or "duties" had always been used to prevent "illegal" trades that would take business away from Great Britain and give it to the Dutch, Spanish, or French. But these new taxes were obviously intended not to prevent trade but to bring in money that was to be spent as the king pleased. And from the beginning the colonists resisted, either by ignoring the taxes, by failure to enforce the new laws (judges and law officers were Americans too), or by open and violent protests.

The government in London, persuaded that it was perhaps not proper to impose taxes that might interfere with trading, then thought of a new form of tax—one that would not touch the shipping of goods in and out of America. This was the Stamp Tax. Under the new law, every document of every sort, newspapers, deeds, wills, summonses, and court orders, had to bear a stamp (to be purchased from Crown officers) before it would be accepted as legal. The men who thought up this scheme never doubted it would be accepted in America and would bring in immediate revenue. Special officers were promptly appointed to sell the stamps and a large supply of stamps were sent off to the colonies.

But the people of America, and particularly of Massachusetts, did not always wait until they had felt the sting of injustice. Edmund Burke, the famous Irish statesman who once served as agent in London for the Province of New York, warned the members of the British Parliament that Americans could "smell out" injustice before it happened. And this is what they did with the Stamp Act. They hanged in effigy in Boston the first "stamp officer" and forced him to take an oath that he would renounce his office. Rather than use the despised stamps, the citizens of Massachusetts stopped printing their papers and closed their courts.

The government in London promptly considered sending soldiers to Boston to protect its officers and see that the Stamp Act was enforced. But Benjamin Franklin, then in London, warned them not to. Soldiers would not put down a rebellion, he told Parliament, but they might start one. His prophecy of course proved correct. But for the time being, the British authorities held back.

When it became clear that the colonists were going to pay no attention to the Stamp Act, when courts continued to stay closed, with men who owed money still allowed to owe it and there being no way of forcing them to pay until the courts started to operate again, Parliament decided to repeal the Stamp Act. When the news of this victory reached Boston there was a celebration such as the province had never seen before. Every church bell rang joyously. Shops closed. Workmen laid down their tools. Citizens paraded through the streets and gathered in the Common to engage in general rejoicing. John Hancock had his employees unload a whole pipe (a large barrel containing a little over one hundred gallons) of Madeira wine on the Common where men and women could help themselves. And that night, from his estate above the Common, where the Massachusetts State House now stands, Hancock put on a fine display of fireworks that sent all the boys and girls in the county to bed that night still staring with wonder. The anniversary of the repeal became a holiday in Massachusetts that was celebrated for several more years.

But when Parliament repealed the Stamp Act, they made it clear that they were not changing their basic belief, that is, that they had the power to pass acts that the colonies were bound to obey, no matter what the subject. And soon after this, Parliament once more tried to demonstrate that power. This time they put a tax on many things that Americans had to buy from overseas. One of these items was tea. England imported tons of tea from its colonies in the Far East and it sold a great deal to dealers in America. And Americans, like the British, were addicted to tea, as a breakfast drink and as an excuse to pause from work in the late afternoon.

Once the tax was placed on tea, however, even though it was so small as to hardly be noticeable, the colonies rebelled. By this time the most ardent patriots—those men who believed that Parliament had no right to lay taxes or other strict laws on the colonies without the permission of the colonists—had organized into a band that called themselves the Sons of Liberty. They would meet whenever they felt some action was needed to uphold their freedom. They celebrated repeal of the Stamp Act and they also planned other actions to defeat the new taxes. Partly as a result of their activities, men and women all over Massachusetts refused to drink tea. If a hostess made the mistake of offering tea to a patriot, he might walk out of her house, or demand she throw the stuff away. Even John Adams, who was one of the leading lawyers in Massachusetts at this time, and a thoroughly law-abiding citizen, asked a lady once if she did not have tea that was "honestly smuggled"—that is brought in without paying the tax—so he could drink it.

As for the merchants who bought tea and other taxed goods from England, they were urged to send them back without even unloading the ships. And a number of the leading Boston merchants formed a Trade Association pledged not to import anything at all from the mother country. When they found a merchant who was buying goods from England, they would send a committee around to visit him, to persuade him that he should stop.

England met this resistance by putting the enforcement of the new laws in the hands of commissioners who were appointed in England, and some of whom were sent over especially to see that duties were paid and no goods were smuggled in from France or Spain or Portugal or the West Indies. The commissioners who came to Boston believed that the resistance came from only a small group of rebellious people who could soon be put in their places. They landed on Guy Fawkes Day, or Pope Day, and were greeted by a long parade in which most of the signs said "Liberty and Property and No Commissioners!" (When the colonists spoke of "property" they meant their right to impose their own taxes and spend their money as they pleased. If the king had a right to tax their property without permission, then he could take it *all* away.)

The commissioners laughed at first but they very soon found out how serious the young men of Boston were. For soon after they had settled down into living quarters, they were visited at night by mobs of young men, some dressed as Indians, who would whoop and throw rocks and make loud threats. And they learned that some months earlier a similar mob, thinking that Lieutenant Governor Thomas Hutchinson had been guilty of favoring the Stamp Act, had broken into Hutchinson's house and completely wrecked it.

There were more disorders now, almost every day, as the colonists expressed their anger at the presence of the

The colonists expressed anger at the presence of British commissioners

commissioners. And the commissioners hired men to spy for them and to report merchants or shipowners who tried to bring in tea or glass or wine or sugar or molasses or cloth without paying the duties. But the merchants either paid no attention to the new laws or refused to buy English goods. One day a merchant brought in some barrels of Madeira wine without paying tax and the Sons of Liberty hauled it through the streets to demonstrate defiance. Then John Hancock had a ship named *Liberty* come in, with a cargo of Madeira wine on which he did not pay duty. The commissioners arranged to have a gang of armed sailors assist them in taking over the ship and sailing it out into the harbor, where they anchored it under the guns of a big British man-of-war.

This deed roused the Sons of Liberty and other patriots to a rage. They attacked a naval officer at the wharf where the ship had been seized, tore off his clothing and took his sword away. Then they found a boat that belonged to the customs commissioners, and they hauled it through town and set fire to it on the Common.

One of the leading patriots of this day, active in the Sons of Liberty, and a member of the state legislature was James Otis, a lawyer from Cape Cod. When the governor of the province, who was appointed by the king, tried to revive an ancient act that authorized "writs of assistance," Otis opposed him. A writ of assistance was a piece of paper that a customs commissioner could issue giving any man the power to help him by searching any stores, breaking into any houses, opening any chests or barrels looking for goods that might have been smuggled. Otis insisted that the British Constitution forbade such practices and he appeared before the governor and the governor's council to make a brilliant speech opposing the use of power in such an improper way. In the course of this speech, Otis uttered one phrase that became one of the war cries of the resistance, "Taxation without representation," he said, "is tyranny!" And most of the citizens of Massachusetts agreed that a government in which they had no voice had no right to take citizens' property away.

But the commissioners continued to press for collection of the new duties and to seize the ships and goods of men they thought were guilty of smuggling. And so the disorders grew. Men suspected of being informers for the commissioners were seized in the street, stripped of most of their clothes, doused with tar, and then covered with feathers—to be hauled through the town on a cart, as an example to others who might be tempted to work for the despised commissioners. And the commissioners themselves received so many angry threats and saw so many demonstrations outside their houses, that they moved out to Castle William in the harbor, where a regiment of royal artillery could protect them.

Among the commissioners and those who agreed with them, there was much talk of the need to make an example of some of the leading "traitors." Among those they counted traitors were Hancock, Otis, and a man named Samuel Adams, who had once been a tax collector and had refused to collect taxes from those who could not afford them. Sam Adams was also a Son of Liberty with a great following among the working people of the town. One commissioner wrote letters to London recommending that these "traitors" be arrested and taken to England to be put on trial for their lives.

But the Sons of Liberty did not consider themselves traitors. They frequently swore loyalty to King George and insisted that they wanted only the same rights as all Englishmen had. Perhaps Sam Adams was the only one who secretly suspected that it was hopeless to expect justice from England and that eventually there would have to be separation. But he did not say this out loud. And the other men sincerely believed that Parliament would be persuaded to grant the rights of Americans to be treated like Englishmen. So when they learned of these letters, they were outraged. James Otis, who felt sure that the commissioners had sent the letters, asked each of them (there were three) to make a public denial. When they refused, he took an advertisement in a Boston paper, in which he declared that the charges were lies and that the commissioners were not to be believed. The day the advertisement appeared, Otis walked into a tavern where Commissioner Robinson and many British officers were sitting and drinking together. Otis walked up to Robinson and demanded a confession and an apology. But Robinson, thinking Otis a mere upstart Yankee, tried to grab Otis by the nose, which was the way an aristocrat in that day would deal with someone he considered to be of a lower class. Otis struck Robinson's hand down with his cane, and Robinson swung his cane at Otis. Immediately the tavern was in an uproar. Robinson retreated toward the back door. Someone put out all the candles. In the darkness. Otis was struck over the head by a sword and seriously injured.

This cowardly attack on Otis enraged the people of Boston still more. Even some who had tried to make peace between citizens and commissioners now agreed openly with the Sons of Liberty. For it was soon evident that poor James Otis had received a permanent injury to his brain. He began to have fits of madness in which he would break windows and fire off his pistol wildly.

The merchants who had agreed not to buy British goods now included almost every shop in town. The four shops who held out were visited by a committee from the Trade Association that soon turned into a parade of one hundred men and boys. When the merchants still would not yield, the Sons of Liberty and others posted signs in front of their shops and asked people to stay away. Early in 1770, a group of boys visited Theophilus Lillie, one of the hold-out merchants, and stuck a post up with an insulting sign on it in front of Lillie's shop. A man named Richardson who lived nearby, and who had worked as an informer for the commissioners, tried to get someone to knock the post down. The boys began to shout names at him. He retreated to his own house and came out with a pistol, which he waved at the boys. Then the young people, with some older men now aiding them, began to pelt Richardson with snowballs and trash from the roadway.

Richardson then ran inside his house, bolted the door, and appeared at the upstairs window. Aiming his pistol with care, he shot a twelve-year-old boy dead. The crowd burst into his house, disarmed him, and almost lynched him. He was taken before the justices and jailed. (Eventually he was found guilty of murder but was pardoned by the king.)

The boy's death created an even greater uproar than did the attack on Otis. Soon afterward, there were more killings that turned the citizens of Massachusetts into sworn enemies of the British troops. For British troops by this time, called because the commissioners felt they needed protection, were quartered in Boston, and even some of the more sober citizens, refused to accept the presence of the soldiers. They were not wanted in Boston, the people said, and ought to go home, or at least go out and stay at the Castle.

Finally an open fight began between troops and some men who worked in a rope-walk. Several soldiers were badly beaten and they and their comrades—there were two regiments of them—swore vengeance on the inhabitants of the town. On a cold Monday night, March 5, under a bright moon, with a foot of snow on the streets, another fight began between soldiers and citizens. It did not end until a squad of soldiers, called out to protect the sentry at the Custom House, who was being hit with snowballs and oyster shells by a group of teen-agers, fired at the crowd and killed five men, including Crispus Attucks. (Attuck was a Massachusetts Indian word for deer.) He had been a sort of ringleader in the fighting with the soldiers and he was the boldest of those who attacked the soldiers at the Custom House.

After the shooting at the Custom House—which became known as the Boston Massacre—the red-coated British regulars were taken out of town and sent to the barracks at the Castle far out in the harbor. The customs commissioners, however, continued to enforce the new taxes by seizing ships and cargoes and the Boston merchants continued their non-importation agreement. At last, pressed by people at home who disliked this interference with trade, Parlia-

An engraving by Paul Revere depicting the Boston Massacre

ment repealed the tax laws, which were known as the Townshend Acts. But the one thing Parliament would not give up on was its insistence that it *did* have the right to make such laws and apply them to America.

And so Parliament made still another law concerning the trading in tea. This was not really a tax law and did not raise the price of tea. Indeed, it made tea much cheaper, so that it cost about half what it used to and cost even less, when sold legally, than it cost when smuggled. For the new law gave to the East India Company in England the right to handle *all* the tea that was sent to America, and this company sold the tea directly to the tea drinkers, through its own agents in Massachusetts and elsewhere. While this really made things easier for the ordinary tea-drinking American, it of course meant that the other merchants got no chance to make a profit on tea and they were outraged. And their customers, no matter how much they may have liked the idea of getting tea for less money, still continued to "smell injustice" in Parliament's making of laws to regulate the lives of Americans. And the Sons of Liberty and their followers joined with the merchants in protesting this new law.

The men to whom the East India Company shipped its tea were urged to turn the tea back, without even taking it off the ships. But the governor would not give permission for this and the tea importers were caught in the middle, afraid to anger the inhabitants by accepting the tea, and unable to secure the proper papers to have the tea returned. The people of Boston thereupon held a meeting—a town meeting—to consider the subject. The Massachusetts town meeting had often been described by visiting Englishmen as the very hot-bed of Liberty (liberty to many Englishmen meant treason). It certainly got the plain people of the province in the habit of voicing their opinions aloud and voting how to order their own town—how to lay out streets, care for the poor, educate the children, and provide the expenses for minister and church. Only men who owned a certain amount of property could vote for the representatives to the state legislature. But any resident could use his voice and his vote in making decisions about *town* affairs.

This meeting in Boston voted to request the consignees—the men to whom the tea had been sent—to refuse to accept it. A message was relayed to these merchants telling what the meeting had decided. The merchants said that they could not refuse the tea. Almost immediately after their reply had come to the meeting, a group of men, all but one of them dressed in Indian costume, gathered at Griffin's wharf, where the "tea ships" were tied up, climbed aboard the ships and, without damaging anything but the tea, or doing violence to anyone on board, carefully and methodically dumped all the tea into the dark harbor. This act became known as the Boston Tea Party. It was not approved of by everyone. Even Benjamin Franklin, acting as agent of the province in London, was dismayed when he heard about it and wished it had not been done. A number of merchants, who were sympathetic to the patriot cause, still did not like to see private property destroyed in this manner and they urged that the men who owned the tea be repaid.

The plain people of Boston, however, and some of the more fiery patriots, even including that very staid young lawyer John Adams, threw their hats into the air (or said they would like to). They felt that this was one more clear indication to Parliament that Massachusetts would never agree that Parliament could interfere in local affairs.

The reaction of Parliament is just what it often is when thoughtless people find they cannot impose their will on others—a violent act of vengeance. The lawmakers in London decided that the citizens of Boston would have to be punished. They promptly ordered the Port of Boston closed

to *all* trade. They forbade the citizens to hold town meetings without permission. They ordered that judges should be appointed in England and paid by the Crown—so they would not be under American influence. They ordered that the governor's councillors—those members of his advisory circle that had always been chosen by the legislature (with the governor's approval)—should also be appointed by the king and be paid from royal funds, so that they too would be free of temptation to vote as the local citizens wanted.

If the men in Parliament had not been blinded by anger and a desire for revenge, or if they had listened to the voices that warned them that they could not do such things to men who were used to thinking of themselves as free, they would not have passed these bills. But no one could persuade the leaders of government that Americans would ever fight back against the organized might of the most powerful government on earth.

One foolish old lord named George Germaine said, in expressing his rage at the violations of "law and order" in Boston, "This is what comes of their wretched old town meetings! . . . These are the proceedings of a riotous rabble!" Said another, even more foolish, named Venn: "The town of Boston ought to be knocked about the ears and destroyed!" And even General Thomas Gage, who had married an American woman, and had spent much time in America, assured the king that the other colonies would not give Massachusetts any help. "If we take the resolute part [that is, act firmly]," said Gage, "they will prove very meek, I promise you!"

Gage and the rest of the loudest voices in London had forgotten the lessons of the Boston Massacre. A show of

A group of colonists, dressed in Indian garb, emptied tea cargoes into Boston harbor to protest British laws controlling tea trade

force did not make Americans meek. It made them angry. And when the Parliament added another law making it proper to move troops into Boston and let them camp and live there, the anger grew to a flame. And the leaders of the other colonies—even those who had been inclined to be most jealous of Massachusetts as the leader in trade—quickly saw that if the Parliament could change the charter of Massachusetts this way, they could do the same with *all* the provinces and destroy local government completely.

The citizens of Massachusetts showed first of all that they knew how to act unselfishly for the good of everyone. According to the law that closed Boston to all shipping, the new shipping port was to be Marblehead, while the new capital of the Province would be Salem. The people of those towns, especially the merchants and the "wharfingers" or owners of wharves, could have made a great deal of money under this law. Marblehead people could have unloaded all the ships and traded all the goods. But instead they invited Boston people to come and use the wharves and storehouses free. Working men of Marblehead offered to unload the ships without pay. In Salem, the holding of all courts would have meant crowds of people who would eat, sleep, and shop there. But Salem inhabitants declared that they would not raise their own fortunes "on the ruins of our suffering neighbors."

Men and women all over America hurried to help the people of Boston, where laborers, ropemakers, sailmakers, caulkers, carpenters, and carters as well as smiths and sailors, bakers, butchers, and all the rest were out of work. From Connecticut, New York, and Rhode Island came loads of corn, wheat, fish, beef, live sheep, vegetables, and sugar. Carolina sent rice. And a gentleman from Virginia, whom very few in Boston had ever heard of, said he would raise a thousand men by himself, clothe them and feed them, and march them all to Boston to help save the town. This man's name was George Washington.

All throughout the colonies, church bells were tolled (with the clappers wrapped in cloth to make a muffled, doleful sound), flags on ships were flown half-mast, and people devoted time to fasting and prayer. What a dreadful mistake the London lawmakers had made about the American "rioters"! Cruel laws and armed soldiers only brought them closer together and made them more determined. Now people everywhere were talking about a Continental Congress that could decide on some sort of union of the provinces so they might act together in their own defense. In every province men and women were pledging to do no business with England. Ladies gathered in every town with their spinning wheels to start the manufacture of American cloth that would make American clothes. True patriots bragged of wearing homespun clothing. Young men met in the public squares throughout Massachusetts to train in marching and using swords, and pikes, and muskets. Citizens subscribed money to supply blue uniforms for the provincial militia. Farmers and villagers began to store up powder, and to make lead balls for bullets, and store them in attics and closets. These were "plums for the British soldiers," for many people in Massachusetts expected that troops would march throughout the province to arrest patriot leaders and put down all show of resistance.

In most of the Massachusetts towns groups of militiamen were formed, each one pledged to supply his own musket, powder horn, and ammunition. The musket of those days was rather like a shotgun of today, for it had no "rifling" inside the barrel—no spiral grooves, that is, to set the bullet to spinning so it would travel in a straight course toward the mark. These guns were "firelocks"—with a contraption, or lock, at the breech that would create fire by the striking of steel on flint. The gun was loaded by pushing a small packet of powder into the muzzle and back as far as it would go. Then one or two lead balls were dropped in on top of that and a small charge of gunpowder was dumped out of the powder horn into a pan near the breech of the gun. When the trigger (or "tricker") was pulled, the lock would snap down, strike fire from the flint, and light the powder in the pan. The flash of that powder, through a tiny hole in the breech, would set off the powder in the barrel, causing an explosion that would send the lead balls flying out of the muzzle with deadly force.

The men who carried these muskets all pledged themselves to assemble at a minute's notice, on the tolling of a bell, or the firing of a shot when danger threatened. They called themselves minutemen. Some of them had had military experience but others had not had too much opportunity to march in formation or learn to obey military commands.

Boston, now closed up tight, with so many men out of work, was full of disorders. The wealthy people were inclined to feel that the "punishment" was justified and they had little sympathy with the patriot leaders like Sam Adams

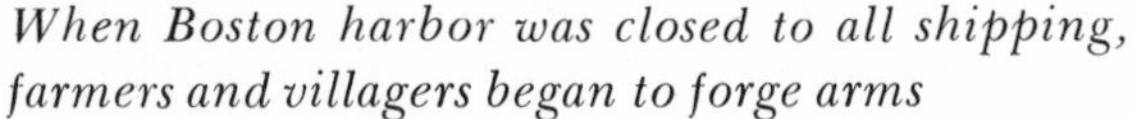

When Boston harbor was closed to all shipping, farmers and villagers began to forge arms

and Dr. Joseph Warren who preached the boycotting of British goods and resistance to the soldiers. But the working people, and even the slaves, who the British thought might be tempted to side with the soldiers against their masters, made life as unpleasant as possible for soldiers, crown officers, and all who did business with England. Men who rented houses to be used for barracks were insulted and threatened. Farmers and carters refused to supply meat and vegetables to the troops. Carpenters who had been hired to build barracks walked off the job. Tradesmen would not sell lumber to the soldiery. Straw meant for beds for the troops was burnt in the streets. Bricks for barracks chimneys were sunk in the harbor. And soldiers who wished to desert—and many were sick of the chilly tents and miserable diet—were encouraged by the plain people, offered disguises and provided with hiding places.

Law officers of the town hardly dared try to punish those who committed acts of violence against the Tories—the people loyal to the Crown—or the soldiers. Mobs would quickly form to free those arrested or to protect any man who had been tied to the whipping post to "get a new shirt." (When a man was whipped across the naked back it was said that he "got a new shirt.") Polite people were offended by the playing of fifes and the beating of drums outside the meeting houses on Sundays, and they were disgusted to see soldiers cruelly whipped, sometimes whipped to death, or hanged, on the Common.

The governor of Massachusetts, Thomas Hutchinson, was replaced by General Thomas Gage, who was also military commander. He called a meeting of the legislature, then tried to cancel it, so the patriots, under the leadership of Sam Adams and John Hancock, named it a "provincial congress" and continued to run the affairs of Massachusetts. They also chose men to attend a continental congress that would be held in Philadelphia. Town meetings, of course, had also been forbidden, but the citizens of Boston got around that by calling a meeting and pretending it was just a continuation of a meeting that had been held before the new law was passed. At this meeting, Dr. Joseph Warren (whom the British called a "rascally apothecary") was to speak about the Boston Massacre. It was said afterward that the British had decided to seize not only Dr. Warren but John Hancock and Sam Adams at this meeting, presumably to take them back to England to be tried as traitors. The Old South Meeting House was crowded and British soldiers jammed the aisles after the citizens had taken their places. Sam Adams, trying to keep the peace, courteously offered to have the citizens in the front seats stand up so the soldiers could move into the pews. But the soldiers had come there not to listen but to act. They were to rush up and seize the patriot leaders on a signal, which was to be given by the throwing of an egg at the speaker by a young ensign. The young man, however, fell down on his way to the meeting, dislocated his knee, and broke the egg. The meeting ended in a rush, when British officers cried "Fie! Fie!" at the speaker and many people thought they were crying "Fire!"

There had also been a great deal of discontent among the soldiers that winter. Many had died, a number had deserted, and most of them were really thirsting for some action. Their officers for a time thought they might mutiny, and they set up cannon facing the regiments, to keep them in order. What troubled many of the soldiers was that they had joined the army hoping to make a fortune in America— in the usual way, by bringing home booty taken from the enemy. But they found they were here merely to do guard duty, to accept insults from the citizens, and to live on short rations. Of course they blamed a lot of their woes on the Yankees, who, according to the soldiers, were upstarts and rebels who did not know their places.

The spirit of liberty, however, burned everywhere in Massachusetts. Even the young boys of Boston did not hesitate to demand their rights. When a certain general, annoyed because they coasted on their sleds down the street by his house, had his servant spread ashes on the hill the boys marched together to the general and asked that their coasting be restored. After listening to their courteous and very logical request, the general had his servant repair the damage. When he reported this incident to Governor Thomas Gage, Gage remarked that this illustrated why it was impossible to beat the notion of Liberty out of the people of Massachusetts. "It is implanted in them from childhood," he said.

And indeed it was. By this time, citizens everywhere were drilling regularly to be ready in case of attack. In Boston, the citizen militia was as well uniformed and almost as well disciplined as the regulars. And military stores were being hidden away in every corner. Bullets and cannonballs were manufactured in Boston and shipped to the outlying towns in loads of fertilizer. There was really no intent to attack the British. But the British themselves were apparently getting ready to make some move against the colonists, as the regiments would go frequently on all-day marches into the countryside. John Hancock became a target for insults from the soldiers, who one night hacked down the fences around his house.

It was soon obvious that the patriot leaders themselves would have to hide, lest they be captured before plans for defense could be made. So Sam Adams and John Hancock, along with Miss Hannah Quincy, the girl with whom Hancock was "going steady," went to Lexington to stay at the home of the local minister, Reverend Mr. Clark. Also in the party was John Hancock's aunt, who acted as chaperone to Hannah.

On April 18, 1775, a young boy earning pennies by hold-

The Green Dragon Tavern was a meeting place for the Sons of Liberty

ing horses outside a tavern for British officers, heard two of them speak of a plan to go out into the country to seize military stores and to capture Hancock and Adams. The boy brought the news to the landlord of the Green Dragon Tavern, which was the meeting place for the Sons of Liberty in the North End of Boston. The landlord in turn informed the patriot "Committee of Safety"—the group elected by the patriot citizens to govern their own affairs—and they arranged to get a spy into the room where the British officers were meeting. They learned the plan of the British but because each one of them was being watched, they could not go tell the man they counted on to carry most of their messages—Paul Revere. The thirteen-year-old boy who had first heard the news was given the job of running up to Revere's house that night to bring the word. Revere had been to Lexington the previous Sunday to visit Adams and Hancock. On the way back he had agreed with two patriot leaders in Charlestown (across the harbor from Boston) to signal them from the steeple of Christ Church—the Old North Church—whenever the British started to move. One lantern would mean the troops were coming by land, the long way, out over the Neck and across the Charles River. Two lanterns would mean they planned to cross over the harbor and proceed to Lexington that way.

Revere sent a close friend of his, one of the men who had sworn to keep the secrets of the patriot meetings, a Captain John Pulling, to show the lanterns in the steeple. He also learned that the committee had already sent another rider, William Dawes, around the long way to carry the message, in case Revere was delayed or captured. Thus, in spite of what the poet Longfellow wrote in "The Midnight Ride of Paul Revere," Revere was not "on the opposite shore" when the lanterns were shown. They were supposed to signal the patriots in Charlestown, in case Revere was unable to get across. But Revere did get across in a boat rowed by two friends that passed very close to the British frigate *Somerset* without being seen. He then rode off for Lexington, after almost being captured by two British horsemen who spotted him on the road. Along the way, he stopped at nearly every farmhouse between Medford and Lexington.

In Lexington, where Revere had to rouse the Clark household from bed, John Hancock was ready to take up a gun and fight when he heard that the British were coming. But Sam Adams after a long argument, persuaded him that if the British captured the two of them, it would be a great defeat for the patriots. The Lexington church bell was ringing and ringing to summon the minutemen from their beds and John Hancock sat polishing his sword and making his pistol ready. Finally, just before dawn, he agreed to go, after learning that a British officer had been inquiring the way to "Clark's tavern." He and Adams made off through the early light to Woburn, where they found refuge again at the home of the local minister, Reverend Mr. Jones.

Meanwhile, the British, heavily armed and warmly clad,

Paul Revere stopped at nearly every farmhouse between Medford and Lexington to alert the colonists

had been ferried across the water and set on land at Lechmere Point, at a place that was surrounded by water when the tide came in. There they were forced to wait and wait for provisions to be brought—provisions that most of them would promptly throw away. Had they been able to leave at once, they might have captured the patriot leaders and postponed the beginning of the Revolution. As it was they had to wade through water that had become almost waist-deep in places before they could start for Lexington.

The midnight bell in Lexington brought the minutemen, some dazed with sleep, out into the chill of the early morning hours. Led by Captain Jonas Parker, some one hundred and fifty of them formed ranks and wondered what to do. After a time, when none of the scouts returned (men who had ridden out to locate the British had been quickly gathered in by the British advance party and made prisoner), the minutemen were permitted to disband but warned to remain within call.

A number went into a tavern to warm their insides with rum or cider and to dry their feet, now soaked with early dew. Some returned home, too far away to hear the summons. And when Paul Revere came back, having been captured by the British and released, there was no force there to heed him. The alarm was not given again until Thaddeus Bowman rode up panting and told of having seen the approaching British just a few minutes' ride away. After him came Benjamin Wellington on foot, out of breath, to say that the regulars were almost upon them. Shots were fired to bring the minutemen back but only about half of them were there, in a single line, when the British appeared in the gray dawn, the new light glinting on their bayonets.

Paul Revere, unseen in the dusk, hastened across the green with a box full of Hancock's papers and heard Captain Parker order his men to hold their fire, and to let the troops pass and show no fight "without they begin it first." This was the only plan of action the rebels had. They were a ragged crew, some of them carrying muskets that looked as if they had not been used in years, and they must have seemed to the well-armed British light infantry as hardly worth noticing. But their very presence enraged the redcoats, who despised Yankees as a race and were doubly angered that such worthless dogs should show defiance of the king. The British soldier, after all, thought of himself as the embodiment of Law and Order and he had been taught to regard as traitors and criminals any subjects who refused to obey the proper commands of men acting in the name of the Crown.

Leader of the advance party of British was Major John Pitcairn of the Marines. When he made out the pitiful collection of minutemen standing there in the gray dawn with their guns at their sides he called on them to disperse and to lay down their arms. Parker told his men to obey the order and the minutemen began to separate, although they all held on to their guns. Pitcairn shouted a curse at

The Battle of Lexington as depicted by an artist of the time

them and asked why they had not put their guns down as he had ordered. Then someone fired a shot. Who fired it—whether redcoat or rebel—is a point never decided. But Hannah Quincy, who watched the action from a bedroom window in the parsonage, said that the British began the shooting. Major Pitcairn, who had told his men not to fire until ordered to do so, insisted until the day he died that the British did not fire until they had been fired on. But he admitted that he had not seen any American fire either, until after the shooting had begun.

The fight lasted hardly half an hour. The British, wild with anger and eager to take revenge for countless insults, rushed like wild animals upon the colonists, heedless of commands, and shot at every one they could see. One of the first shots they fired struck the barn of the parsonage with a tremendous whack. Old Mrs. Thomas Hancock, John's aunt, was looking out the kitchen doorway at the time. "What was that?" she exclaimed. They told her it was a bullet and that she had better keep her head indoors. Soon afterward, two wounded minutemen were carried into the parsonage. One who had been lightly grazed by a British bullet was howling as if death was upon him. The other, shot through the arm, gritted his teeth and made no complaint.

On the green, the minutemen were quickly scattered, all except Jonas Parker, who had sworn he would never run before a British soldier. Grim and straight, with his three-cornered hat full of ammunition on the ground before him, he fired at the approaching British and tried desperately to reload. But a redcoat ran him through with a bayonet and he fell dead on the wet grass. Altogether, eight Americans were killed and ten wounded. Only one redcoat was wounded, besides Major Pitcairn's horse. But the British soldiers ran wild, ignoring the frantic beating of the drums that called them back into ranks. They fired two volleys and pursued the scattering minutemen with their bayonets. They burst into nearby houses and stole everything they could reasonably hope to carry back. Even some of the officers, greedy for the fine plate and cloth they found in some of the houses and avid to discover hidden coin, joined in ransacking the nearby homes.

Then the little affray was over, with smoke still drifting over the green. No one was able to say just what the minutemen had hoped to accomplish, facing ten times their number, and most of them running away before the fighting began. But, no matter how useless and scattered their resistance had been, they had showed the nation that the colonists were now ready to fight.

The British, glorying in their easy victory, gave three cheers, like boys after a ball game, then set out for Concord, while many of the villagers wept at the killing and destruction that had been done. In Concord, the alarm had been sounded soon after midnight, by William Dawes, and men had been working all night to hide the powder and ball and cannon that had been stored there. Nearly all the gunpowder was spirited away before the British arrived and a large number of the Concord fighting men were far from home that morning, getting the military stores hidden in new places. And when the British marched in, with fifers and drummers at the head of the column, only a small party of minutemen awaited them on high ground at the entrance to the village. Outnumbered many times, they turned as the British approached, and marched off in retreat. They, too, marched to the sound of fife and drum, but traveled on rough ground across open country above the road. Each time the British drew near, the patriots retreated, always seeking high places from which they could see what the enemy was up to.

The British found only a few things left behind in Concord that might be useful to the army. They made a bonfire of what would burn and in doing so set fire to the Town Hall, which they put out. They dumped the lead balls they found into a well, from which they were later fished out and used by the colonists. They rolled barrels of flour into the nearest pond, and then started off toward a farm where some informer must have told them other stores had been hidden. They crossed the bridge north of town and proceeded to the farm, where they found only gun-carriages. These they set fire to. Other stores were there but had been carefully hidden.

Meanwhile, attracted by the smoke, minutemen had been gathering from all around so that the American forces, keeping to the high ground that overlooked the bridge, were gradually growing stronger. They were out of shooting range, but near enough to keep close watch on the British. They were outraged to see the redcoats chop down the "Liberty Pole" in Concord and break it up to feed the bonfire. (Most towns had a pole erected to the cause of Liberty and to mark the meeting place of patriots. Boston had its "Liberty Tree.") They were horrified at the manner in which the British soldiers cursed, and the Concord villagers doubled their hatred of the British when the soldiers allowed a Bible to go up in flames.

By half past nine in the morning, there were about four hundred Americans gathered on the high ground overlooking the bridge. There were about a hundred redcoats guarding the bridge while the others were busily burning military goods in the town or at Colonel Barrett's farm. (John Hancock, safe at Woburn, sent a messenger back to Lexington, to ask his aunt *please* to send over the fine salmon they had planned to have for dinner. The fish was promptly sent over by carriage.)

As the Concord minutemen watched the smoke rising, they began to itch for a fight. Were they to stand still and watch their homes burned around them? Colonel Barrett, leading the small force, conferred with the other leaders and they decided to march back into the village or be killed in trying. And thus the decision was made, not merely to stand up to the British, or defend themselves against the redcoats, but to step out and attack them in the open. And so it was at Concord Bridge that the shot was fired that was heard " 'round the world."

The Americans started to form themselves into a column of twos, with drummer and fifer at their head. The British

The "shot heard 'round the world" was fired at Concord Bridge

saw the preparations and withdrew across the bridge, where they lined up in ranks across the road, so that one rank could step back and load, while another moved into their place and fired. As the Americans drew near, the British began to rip up the planking of the bridge. The British, having already seen that Americans would scatter at a show of force, fired a few warning shots into the water. But the Americans, with fife and drum never missing a beat, marched on. Then a redcoat raised his musket and fired directly at the American column. Two Americans were wounded and fell out. But the column neither broke nor stopped. The whole front rank of redcoats then raised their muskets and fired—two Americans fell dead, and several staggered away, bleeding from musket wounds.

"Fire!" shouted an American officer. "For God's sake, fire!" The Americans scrambled to get into position to aim at the British. They were some fifty or sixty yards away, close enough to kill. The first American volley was murderous, killing three men and wounding many, including a number of officers, who were suddenly sprawled on the gravel of the narrow road. The Americans kept on coming, loading as they advanced. The British, with half their officers out of the fight, broke ranks and ran.

Both the Americans and the British waited after that, not quite sure what to do. The British search parties came back to Concord, gathered up their wounded and made ready to march home. The colonists, divided into two forces now, merely watched. But other minutemen were gathering from other towns, and by the time the British had started to march, there was trouble ahead. A mile out of Concord, the British column was overtaken by a new group of Americans. The British rear guard fired. The minutemen fired back. Again the American volley proved more deadly, and the British hurried away, leaving wounded on the road behind them.

All the way back now, the angry colonists peppered the British from every side. In Lexington, the minutemen had gathered again to revenge themselves for the way they had been chased off in the morning. Before the regulars reached the Lexington green, they were almost completely demoralized, shooting wildly at targets they could not see, trying to look every way at once, terrified to see men fall without an enemy in sight. For the colonists were fighting in Indian or ranger style, taking advantage of every bit of cover, brush, tree, fence, stone wall, or farm building, and making no effort to form ranks or columns. This, the British thought, was a cowardly way to conduct a war. But their anger at the colonists soon gave way to panic. Their ammunition—much of it wasted on targets that did not exist—was nearly gone.

In the beginning, the British kept flanking parties on either side of the road, and they occasionally came upon a hidden American and shot or bayoneted him where he crouched. But soon, in the hot spring sun, short of water, without food, and wearied by the ups and downs of the field and pasture and thicket and swamp they had to march through, the flankers gave up and drew closer to the road. There were now four times as many colonists in the action as there were regulars, and had they been organized into a proper army with experienced leaders, they would have trapped the British and finished them. Even so, they very nearly wiped out the enemy, forgetting their own fears in their anger at the cruelties of the British, who tried to retaliate for the colonists' "cowardice" by killing all the males, young or old, in any house from which a shot was fired.

The Americans, although their fire was deadly, were not really such expert sharpshooters as some stories pretend. The smooth-bore musket would not kill a man more than eighty yards away and that did not always shoot straight at any distance. Besides, these were not woodsmen, but farmers and villagers who used a musket only rarely. Their fire was more accurate because they lay or kneeled on the ground and sighted down the barrel, with the muzzle of the gun resting on a stone or in the crotch of a tree or bush, so that it would hold steady. And they fired when they saw a good chance of hitting a man. The British had learned to fire in a manner that was effective against a solid rank of soldiers. But when they could see no enemy, or only glimpsed him in the trees, they had little chance of hitting him.

At Lexington, the panic-stricken regulars were overjoyed to see eight hundred reinforcements, led by Lord Percy, and bringing two small cannon, there to greet them. Now they were able to make a stand, even get something to eat and drink, while Percy's men took revenge by shooting a cannonball through the meeting house, then setting fire to all the houses nearby where snipers might be hiding. The colonists still greatly outnumbered the regulars, and they still refused to come out in a formal line of battle, so Percy very soon pushed on for home, putting the weary troops from Concord up front, where they would be protected, and keeping the cannon in the rear, where it could be used to frighten off the colonists.

Now the constant peppering was resumed, and when the British reached more settled areas, the fire seemed to grow hotter. Almost every house was a small fort, and in some of them the soldiers and the colonists fought hand-to-hand. That the Americans really had courage the British officers now had to admit, for they stood their ground and even ran up within ten yards of the British column, to almost certain death, to fire their guns and shout defiance. British wounded were left behind now for the Americans to gather in, and redcoats who, out of weariness, fell behind the column were quickly taken prisoner. But the "scalping" stories had frightened the British so that many of them fought to the death. Most of those who were taken prisoner found themselves, to their astonishment, treated with courtesy and kindness. The Americans then were still trying to keep war civilized, without wholesale slaughter and destruction.

But the British were now intent on one thing, getting safely back to Boston. Lord Percy had marched out the long way, over Dorchester Neck, through Roxbury and Brookline. He had found the bridge across the Charles partly ripped up, and on his way back he decided to use another route. It is well for the British that he did, for the colonists had an ambush ready. Percy, however, led his weary and disorganized men into Charlestown, across the narrow neck between the harbor and the Mystic River, and he found this way open. Once in Charlestown, he had the heavy guns of the British warships to keep the Americans at a safe distance. When he reckoned up his losses, he found that almost three hundred of his regulars were killed, wounded, or missing. The Americans lost only ninety-three.

But when the British were finally ferried over to Boston, after giving up a plan to fortify Charlestown, they found they were besieged. Provincial troops were encamped in Cambridge, in Roxbury, and on the hills that looked down on the mouth of the Charles River. These were no longer a mere mob of poorly armed and shabbily clad country folk. They were brave, determined, and resourceful fighters. And many more of them were on the march.

Safe in Boston, the British made no effort to break out. Instead, they amused themselves by taking petty revenge on certain dead and living patriots by defacing their property or even their gravestones. They tore all the pews out of Old South Church, spread tanbark on the floor, and exercised their horses there. They used the lumber of the pews for fuel. And they ordered that no one should enter or leave the city on any errand. Later General Gage, at the request of the Boston selectmen, agreed to let men and women go out if the populace would just give up its arms. When the time came to fulfill this promise, however, he had a change of heart. If he kept the citizens there, he decided, the American soldiers would not fire cannon into the city. So Boston was shut up tight.

8 Welcome, Brother Jonathan!

Sam Adams and one or two others, probably including Dr. Joseph Warren and James Otis, had thought for a long time that Massachusetts would not win full freedom until it separated itself from England. But Sam Adams did not say this out loud until the people of America had all been enraged by the cruel laws that Parliament passed to take revenge for the Boston Tea Party. After that, with men and women all over the state expressing their anger at the British tyranny (even in Berkshire County, far out to the west, citizens had refused to allow Crown-appointed judges to hold court), Sam Adams began to tell his associates—men like John Hancock and Sam's cousin John Adams—that America would have to be independent and that they would probably have to fight.

The wealthier citizens, however, were afraid of Sam Adams and wanted Massachusetts to give in to Parliament —to pay back the East India Company ten thousand pounds sterling for the tea that was tossed into the harbor—and to agree to let the king name judges and councillors. Sam Adams found his largest following among the poor—the manual workers, the shopkeepers who were going into debt, the apprentices, the slaves, the servants, the wharfworkers, sailors, and other unskilled laborers—all those who spent their spare time in the North End taverns where Sam Adams was best known. In these taverns, and at meetings of the Sons of Liberty, Sam Adams was able to explain to the people how important it was that they stand together and resist the tyranny of Parliament.

Several times the wealthier citizens tried to have Boston town meetings vote to defeat the actions of Adams. Once they made a special effort to vote down the agreement to boycott British goods (it was called a Solemn League and Covenant). But they lost the vote by a tremendous majority in Boston, and the followers of Adams continued to frighten and punish those who did not join the boycott.

It was a simple fact that the poor outnumbered the rich. And while most of the rich were willing to settle for any sort of government that would let them make money in peace, the poor wanted full freedom—something which many of them had never yet enjoyed. They wanted to decide for themselves what taxes would be levied, whether or not they should serve in the army or navy of the king,

When boycott action was discussed at town meetings, tempers sometimes reached the boiling point

and what church they and their children should go to. Many of the poor, especially those who sailed the trading ships, had been in previous years seized by "press gangs" and forced to join the Royal Navy. And there was always talk of the king's sending in his own bishops to make the Church of England the official church in America.

It was also true that times were very hard, as perhaps they always are, for the poor. Prices were high. The closing of the port naturally put many out of work. In the towns, working men could not trade off hay and grain and vegetables for other things, as farmers could. They had to have money. Even what little money they did get was often paper money that some shopkeepers would not accept at full value. Hard coin was scarce, because the king's officers wanted all taxes and duties paid in coin. In a place like Boston, where trees had always been scarce, families had to send outside for wood and pay high prices for it—or else live in bitter cold.

The poor had good reason to be angry, and they turned their anger against the mother country, and those who took her side. Many a Tory was driven out of his home town and had to take refuge in Boston, where he had the king's troops to protect him. After the Battles of Lexington and Concord, these refugees found themselves tightly enclosed in Boston, along with the six regiments of soldiers and the many patriot sympathizers who now could not get out. All around them were the growing ranks of the provincial soldiers, some uniformed and some not, but all armed. More arms were coming in every day to the provincials. They had almost no artillery at the start, but this soon arrived.

These provincial troops were not all the clean-cut, neatly clothed, tall, handsome young men such as we see today in statues and paintings. Were we to meet a group of them today, we might be frightened at how dirty they looked—hair tangled; bodies unwashed (country people had no servants to carry water and no tradition of cleanliness); fingernails broken and black; hands grimy from the barn, or the forge, or the sawmill, or the cornfields, or the brickyard, or the carpenter shop; clothes worn or torn and loosely fitting and dirtier than their bodies; hats cut or broken or covered with cowhairs from milking. When George Washington saw them, after being given full command of all American troops by the Continental Congress, he wrote home that the Massachusetts troops were "exceeding dirty and nasty people."

Washington was not used to Massachusetts men. In Virginia, he moved among well-groomed gentlemen, who wore white wigs and used powder and other things to make themselves smell good, who had clean clothes and polished boots and glittering buckles and well-fitted knee-breeches. But Washington saw that these Massachusetts people would make good soldiers if they had proper officers.

But officers, before Washington arrived, were not the best. As in all volunteer armies that have not fought together, men became leaders who happened to want the jobs, because other people had no time for them, or because other people did not feel like struggling for such positions. As a result, there were men serving as captains and majors and colonels who knew nothing about war, who were cowards at heart, or who were interested in nothing but making extra money for themselves. It was because of the presence of so many men like this that the next big fight with the British turned into a defeat, when it might have been a smashing victory. But because the British themselves made serious blunders, the defeat in the long run turned out to have been a sort of victory after all. It may even have been the defeat that won the war for America. It certainly won, within a year, the town of Boston. It was the Battle of Bunker Hill.

The battle however was not fought on Bunker's Hill. It was fought on Breed's Hill, the hill next to Bunker's, and it was named after Bunker's Hill just because that was where the Americans had been ordered to make their fort. The American troops were ringed all around Boston—without the heavy artillery they needed to force their way into the city or to destroy the warships that guarded the harbor, but strong enough to keep General Gage and the British from breaking out. Or at least Gage thought they were strong enough. He was essentially a peaceful man and may even have hoped, after the Battles of Lexington and Concord, that peace might still be restored and the two sides reconciled. He had promised the king that "four more regiments" would quickly pacify the country and he had been proved terribly wrong. Now he did not want to make another such mistake, and so he waited and hoped for some sort of break.

He seemed to have got that break when he woke up on the morning of June 17 to discover that the Americans had moved into Charlestown right across the harbor, under the guns of the warships. The British soldiers rejoiced at the sight, even though they were amazed that the fortifications could have been dug without their having noticed them. Now at last they told themselves they had the Americans in a fixed position. Now they could see the enemy and face him in ranks and shoot him down in proper military style. They never doubted that they would drive this "rabble" off the hill in very short order.

Fortunately for the Americans the British failed to notice that the Americans had actually placed themselves in a trap. So hungry were the redcoats for a face-to-face encounter with the rebels—and so slow-witted were the British commanders—that instead of landing on the narrow Charlestown neck in the rear of the Americans and starving them into surrender, they undertook to drive them off the hill.

It was not the hill the Americans had decided to fortify.

It was instead a lower hill, and one closer to the British. Perhaps its being nearer the enemy is what tempted the aggressive Americans to disregard the original plan. But they made a serious error in not placing troops or artillery (of which they had very little) to cover the route over the neck by which the advance troops might have to retreat and by which supplies and reinforcements would have to travel. They failed to put a "reserve force" on hand to take over when the first troops grew weary. They did not bring with them ammunition enough to last through a long engagement. And they had not given thought enough to getting food and water to the men under fire.

As a result, the men who worked and sweated all night, desperately trying to get the trenches dug before daybreak, had to stand there and fight when the British attacked. They had had neither food nor water. The day, when it came, was cruelly hot. A number of the men were forced by fatigue to leave the trenches and go over to the other side of the hill to rest and find a drink of water. There were not enough officers or no properly experienced officers to plan the work and the supplies so that men would not all be worn out digging and would be able to refresh themselves in an orderly way. There was not even a proper plan to set up a breastwork of something more substantial than hay so that all the troops could have protection, and no enemy could slip around to one side and take the Americans from the rear.

Just the same, the Americans fought hard and damaged the enemy severely. The British made unbelievably stupid mistakes of their own. They were the typical mistakes of military men who base their plans on the tried-and-true methods, who do things a certain way just because "we always did them that way." For instance, it was a rule that the British soldier went into action carrying three days' rations on his back. This was a good enough rule when he was marching into a foreign country to fight a distant battle on a field he might not find for two days. But it was silly to weigh down a soldier like that when he was a short march from the battlefield with his campgrounds just across the harbor.

Also the British soldier had been trained to march in a column, two by two or four by four, until it was time to attack and then to open out into a wide front, with half the company in the front rank, and march forward, keeping the line straight. To try to do this in deep grass, through gullies, over rail fences, and up an uneven slope was almost impossible. But the British soldiers, brave as they always had been, tried to do it all the same. Each carrying his heavy musket with bayonet, fully uniformed, with the overstuffed knapsack on his back, they plodded forward to the command, with sweat almost blinding them and the terrible heat taking their breath away.

The Americans grimly awaited the regulars. They had been under fire since the break of day. Warships had bombarded them with heavy shot—some of it chain-shot (two iron balls hitched by a chain) or ring-shot (hitched by a ring) that would rip down trees and kill anything in its way. A number of the militiamen, it must be said, had sneaked away when the British soldiers started up the slope and were hiding on the other side of the hill, in an orchard, or behind haystacks, or trying to get away by crawling belly down in the grass. Some groups were led away by their officers, who were afraid to give orders lest the men disobey them. Some of the "officers" were just good fellows, popular with the troops, who did not know how to take command and force their will on others, who did not want to be disliked and who did not really have the respect of the men they led. This was another trouble with volunteer and untried troops—each of the officers was just "one of the boys" who could be laughed at if he gave sharp orders.

But there was one officer who managed to hold most of the troops right there to meet the British. He was Dr. Joseph Warren, probably the best-loved patriot in Boston. He came to the fortifications with a "commission" in his pocket that made him a general in the American Army. But he refused to take command. He asked only that he be placed in the position of greatest danger. Then he walked about the entrenchments, encouraging the men and urging them to hold their fire until the British soldiers were close enough so the muskets could not miss.

Meanwhile, General Israel Putnam, in command on the hill, had sent his son to summon reinforcements. The fresh troops did not start out for the battle at once. General Artemas Ward, in command in Cambridge, hesitated about weakening his army, for he feared the British might attack there too. By the time he made up his mind, it was too late. And not all the troops that he sent out arrived at their destination. The captain of one group became frightened as they crossed the neck into Charlestown and heard the cannon shot and musket balls whistling about them. "Retreat! Retreat!" he shouted. "We shall all be cut off!" And he led the way in scurrying to safety.

Another company started off and was told by their captain to keep going and he would "catch up with them." He did not appear until they were safe back in Cambridge the next day.

A company under Captain John Chester did reach the hill and go into action. But on the way there, they met another whole company retreating, led by their captain. Chester asked why they retreated. The other captain did not answer. Then Chester ordered his own men to load their muskets and make ready to fire on the retreating soldiers. This bought them to a stop and they joined Chester's men in returning to the battle. Along the way they saw dozens of provincial troops skulking away. Those who

had not been under fire from the warships, as the first troops had been, were terrified at the screaming cannon shot and with no officers to rally and reassure them, they thought only of finding a place to hide.

The redoubt was not at the summit of the hill but at the "military crest," which is always somewhat lower down the slope, so that men will not make targets against the sky when they move around. The new soldiers who marched down the slope were passed by others—some fatigued and staggering from thirst, hunger, heat, and long labor; some

Colonial troops on Breed's Hill courageously faced the onslaught of British soldiers

wounded; others using the excuse of "helping the wounded get off the field."

But those who stayed in the entrenchments, or behind the stone-and-rail fence off to the left, faced the enemy courageously and beat off two charges.

The British had never met such a killing fire. They themselves, "aiming" their guns, as they had been taught to do, by keeping the butt in the hollow between shoulder and chest and then making sure the muzzle was lower than the butt, stopped and fired their volleys without much effect.

But they kept pressing on. When one company had exhausted its fire, they would lie down flat in the grass and let another company pass through. But keeping a straight wide front made them easier targets. And the effort to stay in line, side by side, over the rough uneven ground, wore them down. Finally, they were permitted to drop their knapsacks and charge up the hill in a narrow column without heavy belts and coats. This time they reached the breastwork and were able to get over it and use their bayonets on the defenders. The Americans drove them out of the redoubt two or three times but, with their gunpowder gone, the Americans retreated and hurried back down the other side of the hill and across the neck into Cambridge, with shots from the fleet from the "floating batteries"—cannon on barges—whizzing about them.

Had the Americans had but five hundred men on the safe side of the hill, ready to rush up and fill in when the British came close, and had they had long pikes to push the British off the embankments, it would have been an overwhelming victory for the Americans. The British could not have retreated, because their boats, having landed in Charlestown, went right back to Boston. And the redcoats would have been killed or captured. "Conquer or Die!" had been their order.

The British immediately celebrated a great "victory." And the Americans pondered their mistakes, the cowardice of some, the stupidity of officers, and the heroism of Dr. Warren who died in the redoubt and whose body was carried triumphantly away by the enemy. The American wounded were carried away by the British and landed at Long Wharf, at the foot of King Street in Boston, where they lay unattended all night and many died. Then they were put in jail. Most of them expected to be hanged. More of them died in prison. But General Gage was persuaded to treat the remainder with some kindness—not as traitors but as prisoners of war.

Now it had to be acknowledged that this was indeed a war that was bound to spread over the whole continent. The Continental Congress, meeting in Philadelphia, had named George Washington of Virginia commander of all the troops—and there were troops in Boston now from all over the nation. John Hancock, as the most popular man in Massachusetts, had confidently expected to be elected Commander-in-Chief. He was dismayed and deeply disappointed when Washington was named. But he managed to swallow his hurt pride and bravely offered to serve Washington in even the lowest rank.

Washington was a man who looked and acted like a commander. He was six feet two inches tall. He had a stern face and great dignity, and did not allow anyone to be familiar or offhand with him when he was in uniform or on duty. He gave commands as if he expected them to be obeyed without question. And he had experience enough (he had fought for the British against the French and Indians) to know how to divide an army so that it could be moved around properly and so that his commands would be relayed most quickly down through the ranks. He threw out of the army the officers who had exposed their cowardice at Bunker Hill. He discharged several who were caught trying to draw extra food for their "men," so that they could sell it and keep the money for themselves. And he quickly saw what advantage the Americans had gained from the battle that they had supposedly "lost."

The British, too, on second thought, began to wonder if they had really won. They had taken the hill and fortified it themselves. In a spirit of revenge they had fired red-hot cannonballs from Boston into Charlestown to set the town on fire and had left it a mass of smoking ruins with only a few chimneys standing. But they had lost more than one thousand men. They tried to console themselves that they had faced "three times their number." But this was not so. There were only about one thousand five hundred

Americans altogether who fired at the British. And the redcoats numbered twenty-five hundred. This meant that almost every American gun put a redcoat out of action.

Once they had counted over the true cost of the battle, the British were in despair. Privately they talked of the stupidities and cowardice of some of their own officers—of the men who had been killed through the careless firing of the men behind them, of the terrible slaughter before their commander, General Howe, had ordered his troops up the hill without their knapsacks and in a narrow column instead of a wide front. Until this moment, the British leaders and the British public had been fed on stories of the ridiculous way the Americans fought, of the stupid mistakes they made, of the cowardice they showed, of the ease with which they could be put to flight when faced by a force equal in number. Now it was painfully clear to the British that it was not going to be a matter of turning out "four regiments" and tossing a few extra cannonballs to get the colonists to give in.

In reporting the battle to his superiors at home, General Gage wrote, "The rebels are not the despicable rabble too many have supposed." Dirty they may have been. Ignorant they undoubtedly were. They said "naow" for "now" and "git" for "get." They sometimes wore trousers that flapped loosely on their legs. Some of them may even have resembled scarecrows and smelled like sweaty horses. But they had courage in their hearts, and once they had tasted battle, they lost their fear of death. They would stand and fight to defend their homes no matter how many uniformed soldiers faced them.

But the important lesson that General Gage learned, and the lesson that may probably have signaled the eventual victory for the Americans, was that the cost of attacking a hill fortified by the Americans was far too great in blood and ammunition. The Americans continued to gather around Boston, and finally they started to get the supplies they needed, including heavy cannon, from all over the East. Minor victories against the British were won on the harbor islands and along the coast. It was very plain that the Americans had the British locked in the town of Boston and they expected General Gage to attack them in an effort to break the siege. But Gage held off until it was too late.

The proper moment for the British to have attacked was on January 1, 1776. Had the British but realized it, the American troops at this time were almost in disorder. The terms of enlistment had expired for many volunteers, and they were all engaged in packing up and heading back to their farms. Their places were being hastily filled by fresh troops, newly enlisted, without any real training, with no experience in battle and lacking the habit of "subordination"—taking orders from superior officers and obeying them without question or argument. These new troops might well have been badly demoralized by a strong and sustained British assault. But no such assault was launched.

Instead, an event took place that suddenly put iron in the spines of many colonists who had been dreaming of a peaceful solution. Many of the Americans still had great faith in the king of England, to whom they had appealed for relief from the "usurpations" of Parliament. They expected that when the king sent his annual message to Parliament he would talk of reconciliation, of peaceful discussions and settlement of grievances. Instead, the king issued an angry blast against the rebels and called for severe punishment of all who had dared defy British authority—particularly the town of Boston, of which was to be made an example. What he really required was abject surrender, confession of faults, and acceptance of harsh penalties. His message put an end to all hope for peace in America and convinced most patriots that the colonies must indeed separate from the mother country.

And then, almost a year after the shots were fired at Concord, the Americans made a move that won a bloodless victory—but a victory that had really been won on the slopes of Breed's Hill. On Washington's orders they spent a busy night building a great fortification on Dorchester Heights—a hill that looked over Boston, over the fortifications on the neck, and over the inner harbor. With cannon on these heights, the Americans could demolish the entire British encampment.

Again the British had no idea that the work of fortification was going on. Deep entrenchments were dug. Barrels full of stone and gravel were set in place, to be rolled down on the attackers. Bundles of heavy sticks were laid down to add strength to the embankments. About four thousand provincial soldiers were on hand to defend the place before the sun came up—half of them in "reserve." The British, when they saw what had happened, were sure that it must have taken twelve thousand men to do so much work and do it so well in so short a time. By this time Lord Howe had replaced General Gage in command of the British, and he was just as slow as Gage had been to attack the Americans before knowing how strong they were.

Then there was a stroke of luck that gave Lord Howe extra reason to hesitate. He had put two thousand four hundred British soldiers on transports to move down toward these new entrenchments. A sudden storm came up that made waves so high the soldiers could not leave the transports. The delay gave Howe more time to think the problem over. He decided (very wisely) that his force was simply not strong enough. The Battle of Bunker Hill had taught him that entrenched Americans could not be pushed off a hill without a terrible loss of blood. Never before had any of the British officers seen such a slaughter as on that scorching afternoon in the waist-deep grass of Breed's Hill. It was not a scene they wished to repeat.

And so Lord Howe decided he would let the Americans have the hill. And when he decided that, he also decided he must let them have Boston. For no troops could hold on to the town, with those new cannon ready to toss their shot right down among them, while thousands of troops were ready to enter the town from the other side. And letting the Provincials have Boston meant he must let them have all of Massachusetts. This is what the brave men had really won that June day on the hill they thought was Bunker Hill —freedom for Massachusetts, for all time, from the rule of the British.

On March 17, 1776, the British troops and some thousand Tory families, with only a few of their possessions, marched on board the transports and set sail for Halifax. The Provincials moved into the town behind them. On Breed's Hill there seemed to be a few British guards still standing at the fortifications where so many of the brave had died. But when the Provincials, in their buff-and-blue uniforms, approached closely, they found only straw dummies standing with sticks for guns. And on the front of each dummy was hung a sign, "Welcome, Brother Jonathan!" For the Massachusetts countryman was always "Brother Jonathan" to the British.

Evacuation Day, March 17, is still celebrated in parts of Boston, perhaps because it coincides with St. Patrick's Day. It was celebrated in 1776 all over the colonies. George Washington was given a medal by the Continental Congress for "first putting the enemy to flight." In England, where people still comforted each other with stories of the stupidity and weakness of the colonials, the news of the loss of Boston was staggering and it made more than one or two men wonder if perhaps the whole effort had been a mistake.

In New York, in Virginia, in Maryland, in Pennsylvania, the news was like the sudden rising of the sun. Men who had doubted if they dared support the patriot cause came out now and declared themselves on Washington's side. And

On March 17, 1776, British troops and some thousand Tory families evacuated Boston and set sail for Halifax

new soldiers and more money and more supplies added great strength to the provincial army.

It is strange to realize now that up to this time there had been no official talk of Independence. Even as late as January 25, 1776, the Continental Congress drew up a statement to the effect that they had no desire to establish an "independent empire" but merely wished to "re-establish the constitutional right of the colonies." Of course Samuel Adams had been thinking of independence for a long time. But he was a good politician and did not believe it was wise for Massachusetts to push for independence until the other colonies, through the Continental Congress, had expressed interest in it.

But when the Massachusetts General Court in June put the question to the towns, they discovered that most of the towns were bitterly opposed to any talk of rejoining England. They had seen their "humble petitions" scorned too often and they had felt the hand of revenge and arrogance too many times. One after the other, the towns of the province, great and small, beginning with Boston, called for complete independence from the mother country. And the Provincial Congress therefore petitioned the Continental Congress that it declare the colonies independent of Great Britain.

Promptly the Continental Congress, led by Richard Henry Lee of Virginia, took up a resolution to declare the colonies "free and independent States." On July 4 the resolution, adopted by the Congress, was published as the Declaration of Independence. On July 17, General Artemas Ward, commanding the troops at Boston, received from General Washington a copy of the Declaration. The password and countersign that the general gave to the troops that night were "Independence" and "America." King Street became State Street in Boston and the Province House became the State House. The Kings Arms Tavern

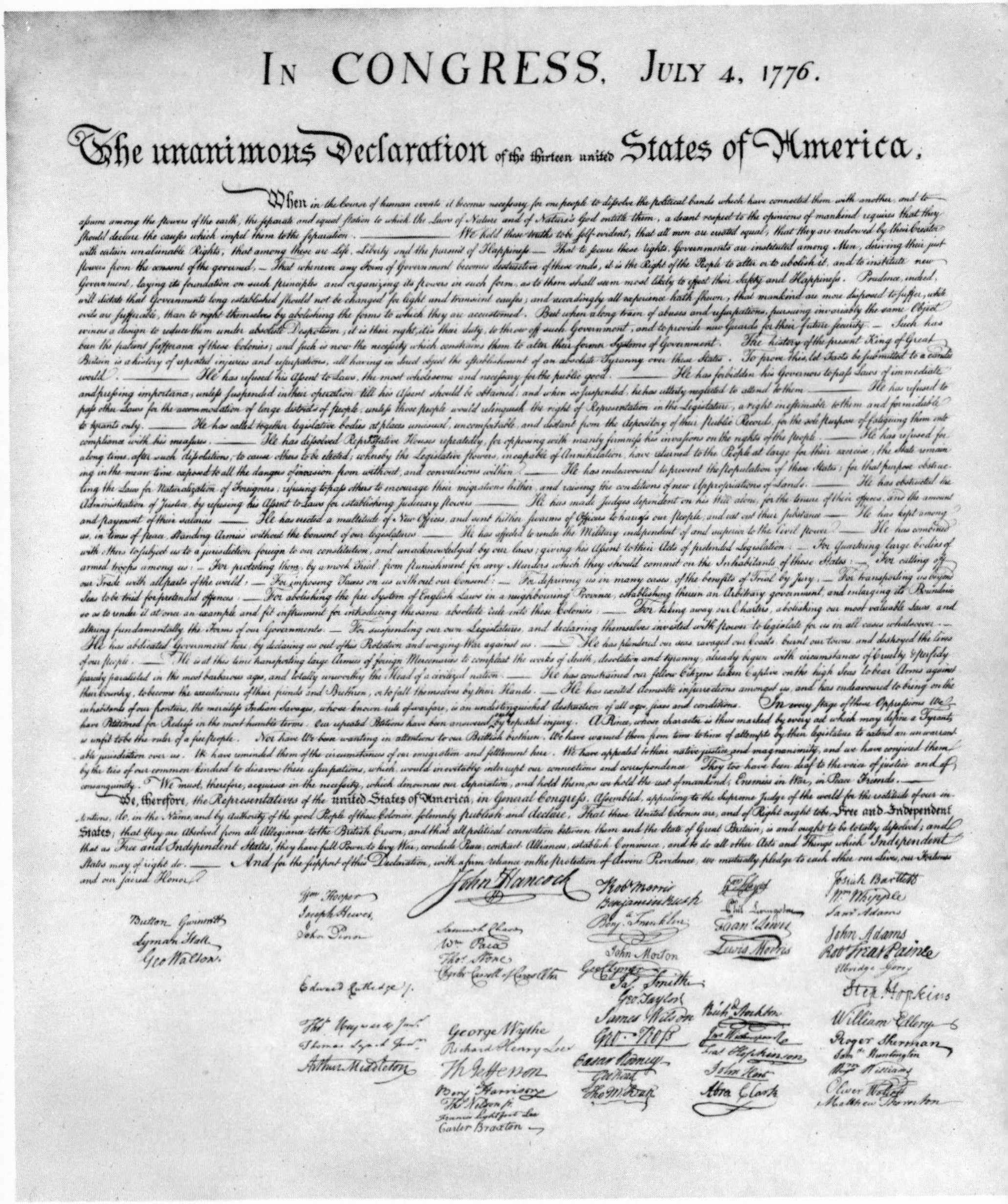

IN CONGRESS, JULY 4, 1776.

The unanimous Declaration of the thirteen united States of America,

When in the Course of human events, it becomes necessary for one people to dissolve the political bands which have connected them with another, and to assume among the powers of the earth, the separate and equal station to which the Laws of Nature and of Nature's God entitle them, a decent respect to the opinions of mankind requires that they should declare the causes which impel them to the separation. —— We hold these truths to be self-evident, that all men are created equal, that they are endowed by their Creator with certain unalienable Rights, that among these are Life, Liberty and the pursuit of Happiness. — That to secure these rights, Governments are instituted among Men, deriving their just powers from the consent of the governed, — That whenever any Form of Government becomes destructive of these ends, it is the Right of the People to alter or to abolish it, and to institute new Government, laying its foundation on such principles and organizing its powers in such form, as to them shall seem most likely to effect their Safety and Happiness. Prudence, indeed, will dictate that Governments long established should not be changed for light and transient causes; and accordingly all experience hath shewn, that mankind are more disposed to suffer, while evils are sufferable, than to right themselves by abolishing the forms to which they are accustomed. But when a long train of abuses and usurpations, pursuing invariably the same Object evinces a design to reduce them under absolute Despotism, it is their right, it is their duty, to throw off such Government, and to provide new Guards for their future security. — Such has been the patient sufferance of these Colonies; and such is now the necessity which constrains them to alter their former Systems of Government. The history of the present King of Great Britain is a history of repeated injuries and usurpations, all having in direct object the establishment of an absolute Tyranny over these States. To prove this, let Facts be submitted to a candid world. —— He has refused his Assent to Laws, the most wholesome and necessary for the public good. —— He has forbidden his Governors to pass Laws of immediate and pressing importance, unless suspended in their operation till his Assent should be obtained; and when so suspended, he has utterly neglected to attend to them. —— He has refused to pass other Laws for the accommodation of large districts of people, unless those people would relinquish the right of Representation in the Legislature, a right inestimable to them and formidable to tyrants only. —— He has called together legislative bodies at places unusual, uncomfortable, and distant from the depository of their public Records, for the sole purpose of fatiguing them into compliance with his measures. —— He has dissolved Representative Houses repeatedly, for opposing with manly firmness his invasions on the rights of the people. —— He has refused for a long time, after such dissolutions, to cause others to be elected; whereby the Legislative powers, incapable of Annihilation, have returned to the People at large for their exercise; the State remaining in the mean time exposed to all the dangers of invasion from without, and convulsions within. —— He has endeavoured to prevent the population of these States; for that purpose obstructing the Laws for Naturalization of Foreigners; refusing to pass others to encourage their migrations hither, and raising the conditions of new Appropriations of Lands. —— He has obstructed the Administration of Justice, by refusing his Assent to Laws for establishing Judiciary powers. —— He has made Judges dependent on his Will alone, for the tenure of their offices, and the amount and payment of their salaries. —— He has erected a multitude of New Offices, and sent hither swarms of Officers to harrass our people, and eat out their substance. —— He has kept among us, in times of peace, Standing Armies without the Consent of our legislatures. —— He has affected to render the Military independent of and superior to the Civil power. —— He has combined with others to subject us to a jurisdiction foreign to our constitution, and unacknowledged by our laws; giving his Assent to their Acts of pretended Legislation: — For Quartering large bodies of armed troops among us: — For protecting them, by a mock Trial, from punishment for any Murders which they should commit on the Inhabitants of these States: — For cutting off our Trade with all parts of the world: — For imposing Taxes on us without our Consent: — For depriving us in many cases, of the benefits of Trial by Jury: — For transporting us beyond Seas to be tried for pretended offences: — For abolishing the free System of English Laws in a neighbouring Province, establishing therein an Arbitrary government, and enlarging its Boundaries so as to render it at once an example and fit instrument for introducing the same absolute rule into these Colonies: — For taking away our Charters, abolishing our most valuable Laws, and altering fundamentally the Forms of our Governments: — For suspending our own Legislatures, and declaring themselves invested with power to legislate for us in all cases whatsoever. — He has abdicated Government here, by declaring us out of his Protection and waging War against us. —— He has plundered our seas, ravaged our Coasts, burnt our towns, and destroyed the lives of our people. —— He is at this time transporting large Armies of foreign Mercenaries to compleat the works of death, desolation and tyranny, already begun with circumstances of Cruelty & perfidy scarcely paralleled in the most barbarous ages, and totally unworthy the Head of a civilized nation. —— He has constrained our fellow Citizens taken Captive on the high Seas to bear Arms against their Country, to become the executioners of their friends and Brethren, or to fall themselves by their Hands. —— He has excited domestic insurrections amongst us, and has endeavoured to bring on the inhabitants of our frontiers, the merciless Indian Savages, whose known rule of warfare, is an undistinguished destruction of all ages, sexes and conditions. In every stage of these Oppressions We have Petitioned for Redress in the most humble terms: Our repeated Petitions have been answered by repeated injury. A Prince, whose character is thus marked by every act which may define a Tyrant, is unfit to be the ruler of a free people. Nor have We been wanting in attentions to our British brethren. We have warned them from time to time of attempts by their legislature to extend an unwarrantable jurisdiction over us. We have reminded them of the circumstances of our emigration and settlement here. We have appealed to their native justice and magnanimity, and we have conjured them by the ties of our common kindred to disavow these usurpations, which, would inevitably interrupt our connections and correspondence. They too have been deaf to the voice of justice and of consanguinity. We must, therefore, acquiesce in the necessity, which denounces our Separation, and hold them, as we hold the rest of mankind, Enemies in War, in Peace Friends. —

We, therefore, the Representatives of the united States of America, in General Congress, Assembled, appealing to the Supreme Judge of the world for the rectitude of our intentions, do, in the Name, and by Authority of the good People of these Colonies, solemnly publish and declare, That these United Colonies are, and of Right ought to be Free and Independent States; that they are Absolved from all Allegiance to the British Crown, and that all political connection between them and the State of Great Britain, is and ought to be totally dissolved; and that as Free and Independent States, they have full Power to levy War, conclude Peace, contract Alliances, establish Commerce, and to do all other Acts and Things which Independent States may of right do. —— And for the support of this Declaration, with a firm reliance on the protection of divine Providence, we mutually pledge to each other our Lives, our Fortunes and our sacred Honor.

John Hancock

John Hancock signed the Declaration of Independence with a bold flourish. His fellow delegates from Massachusetts—Sam Adams, John Adams, and Robert Treat Paine—added their signatures in the righthand column became the States Arms. The British Coffee House became the American Coffee House. And pictures of George Washington replaced those of King George III. On August 2 the delegates from all the new "states" fixed their signatures to the document. Leading all the rest was the big bold signature of John Hancock of Massachusetts.

The Province of Massachusetts Bay was no more. In its place there grew the great Commonwealth of Massachusetts.

Bibliography

CRAWFORD, MARY CAROLINE. *Romantic Days in Old Boston.* Boston: Little Brown & Company, 1910.

HART, ALBERT BUSHNELL (ed.). *Commonwealth History of Massachusetts.* New York: States History Company, 1927–28.

HOWE, M.A. DE WOLFE. *Boston Common—Scenes from Four Centuries.* Cambridge, Mass.: Riverside Press, 1910.

HUTCHINSON, THOMAS. *History of Massachusetts.* Boston: Thomas & Andrews, 1795.

SAWYER, JOSEPH D. *History of the Pilgrims and Puritans.* New York: Century History Company, 1922.

Important Dates

1614—Captain John Smith sailed into Massachusetts Bay in search of good fishing waters.
1620—The Pilgrims landed at Plymouth.
1621—The Pilgrims signed a treaty with Massasoit, chief of the Wampanoag Indians.
1626—Salem became the center for the Massachusetts Bay Company.
1630—Boston was founded.
1675—Metacomet, also called King Philip, organized the Indian tribes of New England against the Massachusetts settlers.
1676—The Indian alliance collapsed when King Philip was killed at Mount Hope, Rhode Island.
1685—James II withdrew the original charter of the Massachusetts Colony.
—The first Huguenot settlers arrived in the Massachusetts Colony.
1689—The French and Indian Wars began.
1691—William III granted a new charter to the Massachusetts Colony.
1692—Witch trials conducted in Salem.
1710—New England troops under the command of Francis Nicholson captured the French city of Port Royal in Acadia (now called Nova Scotia).
1713—England and France signed a treaty acknowledging English control of Acadia and Newfoundland.
1745—Colonial troops led by Sir William Pepperrell captured the French fort of Louisbourg on Cape Breton Island.
1755—The British removed the "French neutral" population from Acadia.
1757—The General Court of Massachusetts refused to allow British troops to be quartered in Boston..
1759—British and colonial forces captured Quebec.

1763–The French and Indian Wars ended with the signing of the Treaty of Paris.

1765–Parliament passed the Stamp Act.

1766–The Stamp Act was repealed.

1770–Five men were killed in the Boston Massacre.

1773–The Boston Tea Party.

1775–British troops marched on Lexington and Concord in April.
–The Battle of Bunker Hill was fought in June.

1776–The British evacuated Boston in March.
–The Second Continental Congress adopted the Declaration of Independence on July 4.
–The Declaration of Independence was signed on August 2.

Places To Visit

Here is a list of several historical sites in Massachusetts that readers may wish to visit.

ANDOVER

ADDISON GALLERY OF AMERICAN ART. This museum is on the grounds of Phillips Academy. Paintings, sculpture, and decorative arts trace history from colonial times to the present. Monday-Saturday except holidays, 9 A.M.–5 P.M. Sunday from 2:30 P.M. Free.

BEVERLY

HALE HOUSE. Built in 1694 by the Reverend John Hale, great-grandfather of Nathan Hale, the house contains many handsome examples of colonial furniture. June 15–September 15. Tuesday-Saturday 10 A.M.–4 P.M. Closed rest of the year. Donation.

BALCH HOUSE. Built in 1636, this is believed to be one of the oldest frame houses in the United States. Mid-June–September 15, Monday-Saturday, 10 A.M.–4 P.M. Rest of year by appointment. Adults, 25¢; children, 10¢.

BOSTON

GRANARY BURYING GROUND. The town granary was located here in early colonial days. Among the many patriots buried here are John Hancock, Samuel Adams, Paul Revere, and the martyrs of the Boston Massacre.

KING'S CHAPEL. This was the first Episcopal church in Boston and later became the first Unitarian church in America. Daily, 10 A.M.–4 P.M.

OLD SOUTH MEETING HOUSE. Built in 1729, it was here that colonial leaders met to plan the Boston Tea Party. Monday-Saturday: June-September, 9 A.M.–5 P.M. October-May to 4 P.M. Closed January 1, Thanksgiving, December 25. Adults, 25¢; under 12, free with adult.

Old State House. This building was the seat of the Royal Governors and Colonial Legislature from 1712 until the Revolution. It was here that the Declaration of Independence was read in 1776, and John Hancock was inaugurated as Massachusetts' first governor. The site is now a maritime and historical museum with reference and photograph library. April 15–Labor Day, Monday-Saturday; rest of year, Tuesday-Saturday; 9 A.M.–4 P.M. Closed January 1, December 25, some other holidays. Free.

Site of the Boston Massacre. The site is marked by a circle of cobblestones in the pavement at 30 State Street.

Faneuil Hall. Mass meetings were held here during the pre-Revolutionary period. The first floor remains a market, as it was in colonial days. Monday-Friday, 9 A.M.–5 P.M.; Saturday to noon; Sunday from 1 P.M. Closed Thanksgiving, December 25. Free. The upper floor houses the Military Museum of the Ancient and Honorable Artillery Company, chartered in 1638 as a school for officers. Monday-Friday, 10 A.M.–4 P.M. Free.

Paul Revere House. Built around 1676, this is the oldest frame house in Boston. Paul Revere lived here from 1770 to 1800. It has been restored as it was during his time, and contains Revere memorabilia. Monday-Saturday, 9 A.M.–3:45 P.M. Closed holidays except April 19. Adults, 25¢; under 14, free with adult.

Old North Church. This is the oldest church in Boston, built in 1723. It is said to have been the site of the lantern signal to Paul Revere to start his famous ride. Daily, 10 A.M.–4:30 P.M. Free.

Boston Common. This is the fifty-acre tract set aside in 1634 for a cow pasture and training field. It remains available today by law for these purposes.

Bunker Hill Monument. This 221-foot granite obelisk was erected to honor the men who fought in the Battle of Bunker Hill, which actually took place on nearby Breed's Hill, June 17, 1775. Daily, 9 A.M.–4 P.M. Closed December 25. Admission, 10¢.

BOURNE

Aptucxet Trading Post. This is a replica of a 1627 trading post. It contains Indian artifacts and numerous relics of trading post days. July-August, daily 10 A.M.–5 P.M.; April-June, September-October, closed Monday; closed rest of year. Adults, 50¢; teenagers, 25¢; 5–12, 10¢; under 5 free.

BREWSTER

Drummer Boy Museum. Among the exhibits are twenty-one life-sized scenes of the American Revolution. Fifty minute guided tours. May 30–October 12, daily, 10 A.M–6 P.M.; closed rest of year. Adults, $1.50; children, 75¢.

CAMBRIDGE

Harvard University. Founded in 1636, this is the oldest university in the United States.

Christ Church. Built in 1761, this is the oldest church in Cambridge. During the Revolution it was used as a colonial barracks. Daily, 7:30 A.M.–5 P.M.

CONCORD

Minute Man National Historical Park. This park was established to commemorate the opening battle of the Revolutionary War. The battleground is near Old North Bridge over the Concord River. In nearby Lincoln there is an exhibit room and several excavated house sites. Daily.

DANVERS

Rebecca Nurse House. Built in 1678, this was the home of Rebecca Nurse, who was hanged as a witch. Listed on her gravestone are the names of the staunch neighbors who vainly testified in her behalf. June 15–September 15, Monday, Thursday, Friday, 1–5 P.M. Rest of year by appointment. Admission, 25¢.

DEERFIELD

Frary House, built in 1685, and Barnard Tavern, which was added in 1763, are interesting examples of salt box architecture. The buildings survived the Indian raid and are now a museum. April 15 until Thanksgiving, Tuesday-Saturday, 9 A.M–noon, 2–5 P.M. Sunday from 2 P.M. Closed rest of year. Adults, 75¢; 7–12, 15¢; under 7 free.

Indian House Memorial. The memorial consists of two buildings, one a reproduction of a 1698 house, and the other a hewn-timber early eighteenth-century house. Each is furnished in its period and includes examples of hand-weaving and pottery. May-October. Weekdays except Tuesday, 9:30 A.M.–noon, 1–5 P.M.; Sunday from 1:30 P.M.; closed rest of year Adults, 50¢; 9–12, 15¢.

FALMOUTH

FALMOUTH HISTORICAL SOCIETY. The collection includes whaling gear, period furniture, and a restored eighteenth-century kitchen. A colonial garden adjoins the museum. June 15–September 15, daily, 2–5 P.M. Closed rest of year. Adults, 50¢; children, 25¢.

SACONESSET HOMESTEAD MUSEUM. This fifteen-acre restoration of a seventeenth-century homestead shows the wagons, furniture, and clothes of the period. May 20–October, daily, 10 A.M.–6 P.M.; closed rest of year. Adults, $1; children, 50¢; no children under 6 years.

GLOUCESTER

CAPE ANN HISTORICAL ASSOCIATION. This museum contains paintings by Fitz Hugh Lane, silver by Paul Revere, fishing boat models, fishing gear, antique furniture, children's toys and games, June 15–October, daily, 11 A.M.–4 P.M. Rest of year, Saturday only. Adults, 50¢; under 12, free.

LEXINGTON

BATTLE GREEN. A monument and boulder mark the place where the Minutemen took their stand. Seven of the men are buried under the monument.

HANCOCK-CLARKE HOUSE. It was in this house, which dates back to 1698, that John Hancock and Samuel Adams were awakened by Paul Revere's alarm on April 18, 1775. Adults, 50¢; under 12, 15¢.

BUCKMAN TAVERN. This tavern, built in 1710, is where the Minutemen gathered before the Battle of Lexington.

MUNROE TAVERN. The British made their headquarters here during the Battle of Lexington. George Washington dined here in 1789.

The above buildings are open April 19–October, Monday-Saturday, 10 A.M.–5 P.M.; Sundav, from 1 P.M.; closed the rest of the year.

PLYMOUTH

PILGRIM VILLAGE. This replica includes a fort-meetinghouse, eleven houses, and an Algonquin Indian campsite, where costumed people re-enact life as it was in 1627. Mid-April–Sunday after Thanksgiving, daily, 9 A.M.–5 P.M.; closed the rest of the year.

MAYFLOWER II. This ninety-foot barque, a replica of the original, was built in England and sailed to America in 1957. Adults, 75¢; children 50¢.

PILGRIM HALL MUSEUM. Built in 1824, this museum houses relics of the first Pilgrims and their descendants. May-November, daily, 10 A.M.–5 P.M.; December-April, Monday-Saturday, 10 A.M.–5 P.M.; Sunday from 1 P.M.; closed December 21, 25. Adults, 50¢; children, 25¢.

PROVINCETOWN

PILGRIM MEMORIAL MONUMENT. This 255-foot tower commemorates the Pilgrims' first landing. Daily: July-August, 9 A.M.–6 P.M.; mid-April, June, September–mid-November to 5 P.M.; closed rest of year. Adults, 75¢; 11 years and under, 25¢.

QUINCY

QUINCY HOMESTEAD. This was the home of John Hancock's wife, Dorothy Quincy. Two rooms date from the seventeenth century; the rest of the house is eighteenth century. April 19–October, daily except Mondays, 10 A.M.–5 P.M.; closed rest of the year. Adults, 50¢; children, 15¢.

BIRTHPLACES OF JOHN AND JOHN QUINCY ADAMS. At 133 and 141 Franklin Street are two seventeenth-century salt box houses. John Adams was born and reared in one; his son was born in the other. April 19–September, daily except Monday, 10 A.M.–5 P.M.; closed rest of the year. For both houses: adults, 50¢, children, 25¢; one house: adults, 30¢, children, 15¢.

SALEM

PIONEER VILLAGE. This reproduction of a 1630 settlement includes dugouts, wigwams, thatched cottages, pillory, stocks, and so forth. June–Labor Day, daily, 9:30 A.M.–6:30 P.M.; after Labor Day–October, 12–5 P.M.; closed rest of the year. Adults, 50¢; children, 25¢.

STOCKBRIDGE

MISSION HOUSE. This house was built in 1739 by the Reverend John Sergeant and is now a museum of colonial life. Late May-September, Monday-Saturday, 10 A.M.–5:30 P.M., Sunday from 2 P.M.; closed rest of the year. Adults, $1; 11 years and under, 25¢.

Hours of admission and prices are subject to change.

Index